Whenever *italics* appear in "Scripture quotations *like this*", the italics have been added by the author, and if italicised material is bracketed inside "Scripture quotations *(like this)*", the entire bracketed section has been added.

ISBN 978-1-7399482-9-0

Cover image: Llandudno - North Wales

Grateful thanks to:

My proof-readers
Jerry Sandy, James Tayler, Grayson Fuhrman,
and especially my wife Margrite.
Not all of them agree with me
on every point of doctrine,
but their comments have been very helpful.

My publisher
Stephen Bishop (www.bible-bish-books.co.uk)
for his guidance throughout the process.

To obtain more copies,
or to send feedback / questions,
email me at: tebboth55@gmail.com.

John Tebboth

THE FORGOTTEN PROMISE

Jesus Christ will return to Earth!

John Tebboth

Contents

Introduction	The book that took 50 years to write	1
Chapter 1	The forgotten promise	5
Chapter 2	An inferior substitute	11
Chapter 3	The real thing	27
Chapter 4	The Lord will have His day	41
Chapter 5	A new heaven and a new Earth	61
Chapter 6	What kind of people should we be?	67
Appendix A	The pre-post debate	79
Appendix B	Could Jesus return today?	89

- *Introduction* -

The book that took 50 years to write

In 1972, when I was 17 years old, I became convinced that God was telling me to write a book about the Second Coming of Jesus Christ. I had become a Christian when I was 13 and soon afterwards, while reading my Bible, I was gripped by this topic (on which I had heard very little teaching) so I left my job, started work as a self-employed carpenter and decorator, and spent at least two days each week working on the book.

Right from the start, I knew God was telling me not to read any books on this subject except the Bible, so all day long, I sat at the desk in my bedroom reading the Bible book by book, making copious notes on anything and everything that I thought might pertain to the Second Coming, and started putting together some chapters for my book. After 15 months of this, with only three or four chapters written, I felt my inspiration was running out and I went back to full-time work. I had no sense, however, that the project had been a failure, as those 15 months of Bible Study taught me so much and became the basis of a teaching ministry I have exercised for many years. In particular, I became passionate about Christians getting to know the *whole* of the Bible rather than just a few favourite verses so, many years later, I developed a course to give an overview of the whole Bible in six sessions.

Over the years, I have taught about the Second Coming from time to time but more recently, the subject returned to the forefront of my mind. In 2018, after teaching a short series on this topic, a thought suddenly came to me: "You will write the book when you retire". This was so unexpected, and seemingly from nowhere, that I immediately told the Lord that if He gave me the strength, I would complete that task… and what you are reading now is the result!

If I had completed the original book, you would now have in front of you a detailed Bible study about signs of the Second Coming (in nature, in society, in the Church, in Israel and the Gentile nations, and so on) and a step-by-step account of what will follow – but there are already many books like that which Christians often find very daunting, especially when they contradict each other! I am hoping this book will be somewhat lighter and of interest to *all* believers (and maybe some who haven't yet put their faith in the Lord Jesus Christ). It is only a slim volume that won't take you long to read and it isn't a thesis on every aspect of this doctrine, but an attempt to *awaken interest* in a topic that so many completely ignore.

I have refrained from detailed exposition of Bible passages and from mentioning all the verses that "prove" a particular point. I have often paraphrased Bible verses rather than quoting them word for word – but I have put all references in footnotes so you can check them if you wish. It is not my aim to *prove* anything but simply to declare *Jesus Christ will return to Earth!*

Having said I have avoided detailed discussion of theological arguments, there are two issues I will mention now, mainly for the benefit of those who are already familiar with different teachings about the Second Coming and might be itching to know where I stand...!

1. I believe that prior to the return of Jesus, there will be a period of unprecedented tribulation on Earth *which Christians will go through* (although many will die for their faith). A widespread view amongst Christians in the western world is that they will be caught up ("raptured") to heaven before this period begins. People holding this view are called "pre-tribulationists", whereas I am a "post-tribulationist", i.e. I believe the rapture will occur after (*post*) the tribulation.

   I know this might put some people off the book immediately, but I want to assure you that my view on this topic isn't very important to its central message and will feature very little – but for those who are interested, I have explained in Appendix A how I arrived at my belief, and in Appendix B I have looked at the possibility that *both* of the above views might be wrong!

2. I believe that when Jesus returns to Earth, He will govern this planet in person, based in Jerusalem, for 1000 years – which means I am a "pre-millennialist", i.e. I believe Jesus will return before ("pre") the 1000-year period (millennium) of His earthly reign. If you've never heard such teaching before and it sounds strange to you, don't worry – just read on! Unlike the pre/post-tribulation issue, the millennial reign of Jesus will feature quite a lot, and I will try to explain why I believe it is so important to my understanding of *why* Jesus is returning to Earth. If you are already familiar with this doctrine but have a different view, I hope you will still read on.

That's almost the last time you will hear any mention of "pre" and "post" until those appendices – so please don't be put off! I mentioned above that when I started on this journey, I was sure God told me not to read any books on the subject, but in later years I believe He showed me this no longer applied, and I did read what others have written. I'm not against reading books (if I was, I would be a hypocrite for writing one), but my greatest desire is that like me you will read the Bible for yourself to discover what it says about Jesus returning to Earth. May God create in all of us a hunger to know more about this wonderful event, and to live in the light of His appearing.

- Chapter 1 -

The forgotten promise

There is a topic mentioned over 300 times in the New Testament – second only to the subject of salvation. All nine writers refer to it, and it is found in nearly all 27 books they wrote... yet, in most churches in the UK, hardly anyone ever talks about it, whether from the platform, or privately – and there are also very few songs about it.

The topic I am referring to is the Second Coming of Jesus Christ, by which I mean His physical return to planet Earth. Jesus Himself promised this on many occasions, and He was not referring to some mystical or spiritual return, but to a literal event so dramatic that nobody will miss it. This isn't because people will see it on television news or social media, but because it will be accompanied by supernatural events seen by everyone, such as lightning flashing from the east to the west, the sun and moon being darkened, and a loud trumpet sound[1] – then Jesus Himself will return to Jerusalem and stand again on the Mount of Olives[2] (the very place from which He ascended[3]). Not only will He return, but the Bible says believers who are still alive will be "caught up" to meet Him as He descends[4]. You might think that such a prospect would be one of the biggest talking points amongst Christians but, as we have observed, this isn't the case. Why not? I would like to suggest several reasons...

---

[1] Matt 24:27-31

[2] Zech 14:3-4

[3] Acts 1:9-12

[4] 1 Thes 4:14-17

We have become too comfortable

The idea that Jesus might return and interrupt our present existence is quite unsettling. Perhaps we are young, looking forward to getting married and having children, and don't want to miss out on things that others around us enjoy. Or maybe we are older, worried we won't finish all the work we had planned to do on our house, or that we will never go on the world cruise we are planning for our retirement. We might even be preoccupied with "spiritual things", such as preaching a 52-part series on the Book of Revelation or working on our church's plan to take the city for Christ. There are so many things that will never get done if Jesus returns in our lifetime.

The same thing, of course, could be said about death – and, whenever someone dies, especially if it is unexpected, we become aware that life here is fragile and brief. If we attend the funeral, someone will probably remind us of this, so we resolve to be more concerned about eternal things, and make sure we are ready to meet God when our time comes – but that doesn't usually last very long. Somebody might even mention the fact that Jesus will return some day, bringing with Him those who have died as believers, but that too is soon forgotten.

We don't think Jesus will return in our lifetime

Already by the end of the New Testament era, people were asking "where is the promise of His coming?"[1]. They had expected Jesus to return much sooner and, because He hadn't, the promise no longer seemed relevant. 2000 years later we may be tempted to think His coming is still a long way off on the grounds that if He hasn't returned yet, He probably won't return for a long time – but there is another way of looking at it…

If 2000 years have passed, His return must be a lot nearer now than it was for those early disciples. If many were expecting it in the first century, *how much more* should we be expecting it? Some will say that in every generation there have been Christians who believed Jesus might return in their lifetime – and that may well be true – but one day there will be a generation who believe this and *will be right*. That generation could be us.

We are busy living for Christ here and now

Living for Christ now may sound like a very laudable reason for not thinking about His return. There is so much to be done in our own lives – and those around us (both believers and unbelievers) need so much help – so why think about the future when we have pressing issues in the present?

There have, of course, been some extremists who became so obsessed with their belief that Jesus was about to return that they withdrew from everyday life to await that event – only to be disappointed – so we do need a balance here. Yes, we need to be living for Christ here and now – bringing

[1] 2 Pet 3:4

glory to Him in our homes, churches and places of work – but we also need a goal beyond this. If someone spends all their life improving their home but dies before they have time to enjoy living in it and has no-one to whom they want to leave the property, most of us would consider that a rather sad existence. Or think of somebody who works long hours for their employer with little reward and no prospect of becoming a shareholder – what's the point?

Many Christians are embarrassed to talk about earning rewards (you may have heard some say, "I'm happy to serve the Lord even if I get nothing in return"!), but this isn't a Biblical stance. Take, for example, the faithful Christian worker who is seeking to help others in their walk with Christ: Peter tells them "when the Chief Shepherd appears, you will receive the crown of glory that will never fade away"[1]. So, he doesn't say they should stop their present work, but he tells them to have an eye on the future when they will be rewarded. We will say more about rewards in the next chapter.

We are more interested in "the last days"

There are a few Christians, and some churches, who seem to be *very* interested in the return of Jesus – but, when we listen carefully to what they are saying, we often find they are more concerned with what will happen *before* He returns than what will happen *when* He returns. Maybe they focus on the world, and can tell us all about a cashless society, microchips embedded in people's hands, and planes crashing because the pilot has been snatched away to meet the returning Jesus – or maybe they focus on the

[1] 1 Pet 5:4

church, and talk about great outpourings of the Spirit and worldwide revival – but, either way, they say little or nothing about *why* Jesus is returning, and what He will do *when* He returns. It's like a couple planning to get married and talking incessantly about all that must be done before the wedding, but never giving any thought to the wedding itself, or their plans and expectations for married life.

Interestingly enough, the few chapters of the book that I wrote in 1972 were all about things that would happen *before* the return of Jesus – what the world will be like, what the political scene will be, what will be happening in the "true church" and in the "false church", etc. I'm not saying these things aren't important, and certainly the Bible has much to say about them, but they won't be the emphasis of this book.

We think the subject is too complex

Some preachers never tackle the subject of the Second Coming because they think it's too complex or controversial, and the average Christian is completely baffled by terms like "pre-tribulation" or "post-millennial". These terms are important and, as I mention in the introduction to this book, I do have definite views about the theories they describe – but when I first teach a group of people about the Second Coming, I tend to avoid the complications and simply concentrate on the wonderful fact that Jesus will return. On the whole, I will also be avoiding such issues in this book but, for those who want to know more, will deal with some of them in the appendices.

As I said, the return of Jesus is mentioned over 300 times in the New Testament and, although some of the passages *are* difficult to understand, *most of them are not*. Many simply remind us that He will return, and experience certainly says we need a lot of reminding!

We don't see the point of Jesus returning

This might shock you, and few would admit it, but I've become increasingly convinced that many Christians don't see the point of Jesus returning to Earth. Many have the idea He is coming simply to snatch us away to heaven and destroy the present world so, since we are going to heaven when we die, why not let us do all the things we had planned to do first, then go to heaven after that?

Some stress that Jesus is coming to judge the world but if, as many believe, unbelievers go to hell when they die, what difference will the Second Coming make to them?

My conviction, however, is that Jesus is returning to Earth to do a number of things that (a) He didn't do on His first visit and (b) *won't* be achieved by us dying and going to heaven. But, before I move on to that, I need to explain why dying and going to heaven is *not* our supreme hope.

- *Chapter 2* -
An inferior substitute

When Christians miss an important Biblical truth, they tend to substitute something else.

Suppose for example, we don't baptise new believers by full immersion in water as the Scriptures teach – what will we do with the many verses about baptism? Some Christians choose to ignore them completely, but most sprinkle some water on the head of a baby or an adult and call it baptism (even though the word itself indicates a total immersion). Or suppose that, like most Christians in the West, we aren't being persecuted – what will we do with the many verses about suffering for our faith? What many do is apply them to sickness and infirmity of the body, even though this comes to nearly everyone and there is no choice about it, whereas suffering for Christ is a choice. I'm not saying there is nothing to learn from sickness (quite the reverse), but it can't be equated with suffering for our faith.

What is our ultimate goal?

In a similar way, we know the Bible has a lot to say about some sort of ultimate goal of our faith; we believe that what we have now is only a foretaste of something far better to come – but what is it?

For most Christians in the West, it is to die and go to heaven, so at funerals we nearly always hear at least one of these statements about the deceased, based on verses from the New Testament...

"They have entered into their reward"[1]

"They have received the crown of righteousness"[2]

"They have heard the words of Jesus 'Well done, good and faithful servant'"[3]

"Death has been swallowed up in victory"[4]

... yet if we read the verses in context, we find that *not one of them* refers to death, but to the Second Coming of Jesus! I vividly recall attending a Christian burial in a Pakistani village and the Second Coming was mentioned over and over again – but in British funerals I am sad to say the topic rarely gets a mention.

When Paul received good news about the Thessalonian church he founded, he wrote that everyone was talking about their faith and how they had "turned to God from idols to serve the true and living God, and to *wait...*" for what? For death, so they could go to heaven and be with Jesus? No! "... to wait for His Son *from* heaven"[5] – and if we continue to read the letter, we find that all five chapters end with an encouragement to look forward to the return of Jesus. Then, in the second letter, Paul writes about the persecutions and trials the Thessalonians were enduring, but says God will redress the balance – when and where? In heaven? No! ... again, he points them to the day when "the Lord Jesus is revealed *from* heaven"[6].

---

1 Matt 16:27
2 2 Tim 4:8
3 Matt 25:19-23
4 1 Cor 15:54
5 1 Thes 1:9-10
6 2 Thes 1:4-7

Another popular quotation at funerals is Jesus' statement that He was going to prepare a place for us in His Father's house – but He continues "and if I go and prepare a place for you, *I will come back*..."[1]. When He ascended to heaven, the angels reminded His disciples of that promise "why do you stand here looking into the sky? This same Jesus, who has been taken from you into heaven, *will come back*..."[2].

His final message in Scripture is "I am coming soon". Is our reply "not yet Lord!" or "I'll see you in heaven first" ... or is it the conclusion of that verse "Amen. Come, Lord Jesus"[3]?

Treasure and rewards in heaven?

But surely, some may object, there are many verses about treasure and rewards in heaven. Yes, there are, and as we said in the previous chapter, we shouldn't downplay the importance of rewards. Didn't Jesus say of those who are persecuted for His sake "great is your reward in heaven"[4], and didn't He promise the rich young ruler that, if he gave everything to the poor and followed Him, He would have treasure in heaven[5]? I agree that if we take these verses on their own, we might get the impression that heaven is our ultimate destiny where we will reap these benefits – but we always need to search the Scriptures to get the whole picture.

---

[1] John 14:2-3
[2] Acts 1:11
[3] Rev 22:20
[4] Matt 5:12
[5] Mark 10:21

Jesus told us to store up treasures in heaven "where moth and rust do not destroy, and where thieves do not break in and steal"[1] which suggests heaven is a safe storage place, better than any bank on Earth. Paul certainly agreed and wrote to Timothy "He is able *to guard* what I have entrusted to Him" but he added the phrase *"for that day"*[2] – raising the question "for which day?". At the time, Paul was expecting imminent execution and, later in the letter, he wrote "now there is *in store for me* the crown of righteousness, which the Lord, the righteous Judge, will award to me on *that day"*. Did he think that day would be in a few weeks' time when he expected to die and go to heaven? No! Paul clarifies what he means by adding "...not only to me, but also to all who have longed for *His appearing*"[3].

Peter also wrote about "an inheritance that can never perish, spoil or fade – *kept in heaven* for you, who through faith are shielded by God's power *until the coming of the salvation ready to be revealed in the last time*" ... and then goes on to refer to the time "when Jesus Christ is revealed"[4].

These passages bring me to the conclusion that treasure and rewards are earned by our service for the Lord while we are here on Earth but stored in heaven's bank until Jesus returns and we reap the ultimate benefits. After all, if someone keeps their earthly treasure in a bank, they don't expect to spend their retirement in the vault looking at it – they hope the day will come when they can withdraw their savings, or sell those gold bars, and enjoy a world cruise!

---

[1] Matt 6:20

[2] 2 Tim 1:12

[3] 2 Tim 4:8

[4] 1 Pet 1:4-7

Jesus Himself linked the distribution of rewards with His return in two similar parables about money – talents[1] and minas[2]. In each story, the servants were told to trade while the Master was away, then when He returned, the profitable traders were rewarded. Jesus didn't explain either of these parables but He once told a Pharisee to give to the poor and disabled, concluding "although they cannot repay you, you will be repaid *at the resurrection of the righteous*"[3]. On another occasion, He clearly said "the Son of Man is going to come in His Father's glory with His angels, and *then* He will reward each person according to what he has done"[4] and, in His final message to mankind that we mentioned earlier, He said "Behold, I am coming soon! My reward is with Me, and I will give to everyone according to what he has done"[5].

Death is an enemy

Another phrase we may hear at funerals is *"death has lost its sting"*[6] – but is that true? Although we can (and should) rejoice when a believer goes to heaven, it can still be very painful for those left behind. We might comfort ourselves by thinking we will see them again when we die – but that will only leave others grieving for us. Will this cycle never end? Will there ever be a time when we are *all* united again? The wonderful answer is yes, when Jesus returns, but until that day, death is *still an enemy*. Scripture says it will be the *last*

---

[1] Matt 25:14-30
[2] Luke 19:11-27
[3] Luke 14:14
[4] Matt 16:27
[5] Rev 22:12
[6] 1 Cor 15:55

enemy to be destroyed, but that won't happen until Christ returns[1].

The first Christian martyr Stephen had a wonderful entrance to heaven and those nearby heard him say "I see heaven open and the Son of Man standing at the right hand of God"[2] – yet we read that "godly men mourned deeply for him"[3]. Later, a disciple called Dorcas who was always doing good and helping the poor became sick and died and, when Peter arrived, he found a room full of people crying. He didn't rebuke them for this or tell them Dorcas had received a rich reward in heaven but raised her from the dead[4]. I'm not suggesting that should be our usual expectation, and indeed, Paul's letter to the Thessalonians talks about believers who had died – but how does he comfort those left behind? Did he say, as we often do, *"you will see your loved one again in heaven"*? No – he makes no mention of heaven, but writes…

> "We do not want you to be ignorant about those who fall asleep, or to grieve like the rest of men, who have no hope. We believe that Jesus died and rose again and so we believe God *will bring with Jesus* those who have fallen asleep in Him"[5]

Once again, he is clearly talking about the Second Coming! I am *not* saying we *won't* see those already in heaven when

---

[1] 1 Cor 15:22-26
[2] Acts 7:56
[3] Acts 8:2
[4] Acts 9:36-42
[5] 1 Thes 4:13-14

we die (although the Scriptural evidence for this is somewhat scant), but I *am* saying that's *not* what we are told to look forward to. We await the day when, not only will Jesus return to this planet, but He will bring with Him all believers who have died – which is much better than heaven because we will *all* be together and death will be no more.

To be like Jesus

Surely the longing of every Christian is to be like Jesus – free from sin, free from the weaknesses of the flesh, and perfectly reflecting Him – but when will this be fully achieved? Again, the usual answer is "when we die and go to heaven" … yet John writes "when He *appears*, we shall be like Him"[1].

A favourite text about heaven that Christians like to quote is "our citizenship is in heaven" but it's not even the whole verse, which continues "and we eagerly await a Saviour *from there*, the Lord Jesus Christ". Then, if we read further still, we find out one important reason why the Second Coming, rather than heaven, should be the focus of our expectation of becoming like Jesus … "who, by the power that enables Him to bring everything under His control, will transform *our lowly bodies* so that they will be like His glorious body."[2] To put it simply, we can never be perfectly like Jesus until we have a body like His resurrection body.

When we die, our spirits will go to heaven, but our bodies will rot in the grave or be burned. Many Christians are content with that arrangement (good riddance to our

[1] 1 John 3:2
[2] Phil 3:20-21

troublesome flesh!) but is that how we should view the body God gave us, about which David wrote that we are "fearfully and wonderfully made"[1]? Job had every reason to be eager to get rid of his flesh that was covered with painful sores from head to foot[2] – but, although he recognised it would eventually be destroyed, he looked forward to a day when *in his flesh* he would see God… a time he described as "the end" when his Redeemer would stand on Earth[3]. In the Old Testament, we find very little understanding of life immediately after death (which is why Paul wrote to Timothy that Jesus "brought life and *immortality* to light through the gospel"[4]) but there *was* an awareness of a future resurrection. Daniel as well as Job specifically referred to it[5] but it wasn't just these well-known characters. The writer to the Hebrews names many heroes of the faith and then refers to women who "received back their dead, raised to life again" (which happened in the ministries of Elijah and Elisha[6]). We can be confident that those raised in these incidents eventually died again, but the writer continues "others were tortured and refused to be released, so that they might gain a *better resurrection*"[7]. Surely this better resurrection to which this crowd of unnamed Old Testament believers looked forward was the same hope that Job and Daniel expressed.

When we come to the New Testament, we find that belief in a future resurrection was widespread. Although rejected by

---

1 Psa 139:14
2 Job 2:7
3 Job 19:25-27
4 2 Tim 1:10
5 Dan 12:2,13
6 1 Kings 17:22; 2 Kings 4:35
7 Heb 11:35

the Sadducees, it was taught by the Pharisees[1] and endorsed by Jesus[2]. Martha the sister of Lazarus said "I know he will rise again in the resurrection at the last day"[3]. Maybe, however, the most surprising statement on this topic was made by Paul when he appeared before the Jewish Sanhedrin and said "I stand on trial because of my hope in the resurrection of the dead"[4]. I wonder how many Christians today facing any sort of trial would say that – they might well speak about life after death, but *resurrection of the dead*?

In case anyone should think Paul was referring only to some sort of spiritual resurrection (like going to heaven when we die), we should note his prayer for the Thessalonians that "spirit, soul *and body* be kept blameless at the coming of our Lord Jesus Christ"[5]. The risen Jesus was careful to show His disciples that He was more than a spirit – He was *flesh and bones* – He told them to touch Him, and He ate a piece of fish in front of them all[6]. Not only did this show that *He* had risen bodily but illustrated *our* ultimate destiny when our bodies will be like His.

Just a seed

The body of Jesus after His resurrection had both similarities and differences compared to the one He had before. For one thing, people often failed to recognise Him[7]

---

[1] Acts 23:8
[2] Matt 22:30-32
[3] John 11:24
[4] Acts 23:6
[5] 1 Thes 5:23
[6] Luke 24:37-42
[7] Luke 24:16; John 20:14, 21:4

– yet a brief action or a few words convinced them it really was Jesus[1]. Then, this risen Jesus twice appeared in a room where the doors were locked[2], and He could also disappear[3] – there is no record of such events before His crucifixion but, after the resurrection, it happened repeatedly over nearly six weeks[4]. Similarly, our resurrection bodies will be in some ways like our present ones but, in other ways, far superior.

The Apostle Paul describes our present body as a "seed" which is planted when we die, but later raised as something more glorious – not in heaven, but when the last trumpet sounds and all the dead are raised[5]. Paul knew nothing about DNA of course, but modern science has shown that a tiny DNA sample (a seed) contains our whole genetic code. Hence it doesn't matter whether our bodies rot in the ground over a period of time or are destroyed beyond recognition in a fire... God can take a seed and from it create our resurrection body. Having said that, both Jews and Christians have traditionally preferred burial to cremation but that has changed in recent years. I want to emphasise that I do not believe this has any effect on our eternal destiny (if that was the case, many famous martyrs who were burned at the stake would be lost!) but, for me, cremation can send out a message that God has no further use for my body, whereas burial can be a statement of faith that He does.

---

1 Luke 24:30-31; John 20:16, 21:6-7

2 John 20:19,26

3 Luke 24:31

4 Acts 1:3

5 1 Cor 15:35-55

But what about believers already in heaven?

Before we close this chapter, we must answer the question "but what about my loved ones who have died and gone to heaven – what is their experience?".

It may come as a surprise to learn that the Bible tells us very little about this, and far more about what will happen to them when Jesus returns. Many of the verses people quote in regard to heaven aren't about heaven at all! Take, for example, "the wolf will live with the lamb" (sometimes used to prove there are animals in heaven) – but the context tells us this will happen when the *Earth* is full of the knowledge of the LORD[1]. Then some will quote "He will wipe every tear from their eyes"[2] and other verses from Revelation 21 – but the whole chapter is about a *new Earth* to be created after the first heaven and first Earth have passed away[3].

Then, a further surprise is that heaven isn't a place of absolute bliss where believers are free from all concern. The book of Revelation gives us a glimpse of martyrs in heaven (of whom Stephen was the first) calling out in a loud voice "How long, Sovereign Lord, holy and true, until You judge the inhabitants of the Earth and avenge our blood?" and the answer is they must wait a little longer *until the number of martyrs is completed*[4]. They are concerned (even distressed?) that despite their faithful witness unto death, the Earth is still in rebellion against God, but they *like us* are pointed to a time when there will be no more martyrs.

---

[1] Isa 11:6-9
[2] Rev 21:4
[3] Rev 21:1
[4] Rev 6:9-11

We do, however, know a few simple facts about believers who have gone to heaven which should be enough to give us complete rest and assurance:

1. Dead believers are *with Christ*[1]. As Jesus said to the thief on the Cross "today you will be *with Me* in Paradise"[2]. I clearly remember the first Christian friend to die after I became a believer. Ted was in his mid-40s when he suffered a massive heart attack and, for several days, was in a coma in hospital. His wife and sister were at his bedside praying for healing when Ted regained consciousness for a few minutes and said "I've seen Jesus! They've let me come back to tell you how wonderful He is". Immediately his wife and sister stopped praying for recovery and said "Lord, you can take him. We don't want to keep him here for ourselves" ... and shortly afterwards, Ted died and has been with Jesus ever since. If we could grasp just something of the wonder of this truth alone, we wouldn't be so anxious to know more.

2. Because dead believers are with Christ, to die is *gain* and *far better*[3]. Just consider that... not a little better, or quite a lot better, but *far better* (the literal meaning is "very much for more better")!

3. Dead believers are *not dead*! The Bible contains many examples of dead believers appearing and/or speaking – such as Samuel[4], Moses and Elijah[5], the dead saints

---

[1] Phil 1:23
[2] Luke 23:43
[3] Phil 1:21-23
[4] 1 Sam 28:11-14
[5] Matt 17:3

who rose when Jesus was crucified[1], and the martyrs in heaven[2]. Jesus Himself said that Abraham, Isaac and Jacob are still alive[3], and that anyone who believes in Him will never die[4].

We should mention at this point that some of the above people, such as Moses and Elijah, appeared on Earth in a recognisable form, suggesting they already had their resurrection bodies – but these are clearly exceptional cases and shouldn't be used as a basis of belief. I do think it is reasonable, however, to assume that people in heaven can recognise each other just as Peter recognised Moses and Elijah when Jesus was transfigured.

4. Dead believers are *asleep*, as the New Testament repeatedly asserts[5]. As shown above, this doesn't mean they have no consciousness but, if someone is asleep rather than dead, you expect them to wake up again! That's why Jesus said that Lazarus[6] and Jairus' daughter[7] were "asleep" although actually they were both dead. Being asleep may be very pleasant, but it isn't the ultimate reality – we often describe this life as temporary and life after death in heaven as permanent, but the truth is that *both are temporary arrangements*.

   One interesting feature of natural sleep is dreaming and, without building a doctrine around it, this may give us

---

[1] Matt 27:52-53

[2] Rev 6:10

[3] Luke 20:37-38

[4] John 11:25-26

[5] Acts 7:60, 13:36; 1 Cor 11:30, 15:6, 18, 51; 1 Thes 4:13-15, 5:10

[6] John 11:11

[7] Mark 5:39

some insight into the heavenly state. In dreams there are no restrictions of time and space – people and events from different eras and places can all be blended together – I once dreamed that C.H.Spurgeon (who died in 1892) came to a Christian holiday venue where I was speaking (but he spoke first then no-one stayed to listen to me)! A dream may cover weeks or even years but, when we wake up, we may find we only dropped off for 20 minutes.

Our problem is that because *we* are so taken up with our lives *here and now*, we want to know what our departed loved ones are doing *here and now* but fail to realise they are in a different realm. Some believers have been "asleep in Jesus" (although fully conscious) for centuries but when they awake maybe it will seem like a few moments and we will all see Jesus, and one another, "in real time"!

5. When Jesus returns, those who are still alive "will *certainly not* precede those who have fallen asleep" because "the dead in Christ *will rise first*"[1]. The purpose of this book is to inspire Christians to look forward to the return of Jesus, seeing it as their supreme hope, but what if we die first – will we have missed out? Certainly not! The verse I have quoted means that believers who have died won't be treated as second class citizens but will have the grandstand view!

---

[1] 1 Thes 4:15-16

And what about the unbelievers?

Finally, I will mention the sad and terrifying truth that even hell is a place for bodies – Jesus said "be afraid of the One who can destroy both soul *and body* in hell"[1]. Jesus, Daniel and Paul all spoke of a resurrection of both the righteous *and* the unrighteous[2], and this should make us realise just how important our bodies are to God – not only now but in the age to come. It is in our bodies that we have lived to please or reject Him and it is in our bodies that we will reap the reward, whether good or bad.

This means that just as death isn't the door to the believer's ultimate destiny, neither is that true of the unbeliever. If, as we have seen, hell is a place for bodies, this means no unbeliever has gone there yet – something Jesus confirmed on several occasions. In the parables of the weeds and of the dragnet, for example, He refers to the wicked being thrown into the fiery furnace "at the end of the age".[3] His teaching about the sheep and the goats begins with the words "when the Son of Man comes in His glory", and ends "*then* they *(the goats)* will go away to eternal punishment, but the righteous to eternal life". Paul also says that is only after Jesus is revealed from heaven in blazing fire that the unrighteous "will be punished with everlasting destruction"[4]. In Revelation we read about the final judgment occurring after Earth and sky have vanished and "if anyone's name was not found written in the book of life, he was thrown into the lake of fire"[5]. John refers to this lake

---

[1] Matt 10:28

[2] Dan 12:2; John 5:28-29; Acts 24:15

[3] Matt 13:40-42, 49-50

[4] 2 Thes 1:9

[5] Rev 20:11-15

of fire as "the *second* death" – something far worse than the first.

The only Bible passage that might lead us to think unbelievers are already in hell is Jesus' teaching about the rich man and Lazarus[1], in which the rich man dies and is immediately "in torment" – but there are two possible explanations for this. First, it could simply be an illustration in which Jesus merges the present age with future judgment in order to make His point. A more likely explanation, however, lies in the fact that the word translated "hell" in many English versions is the Greek "hades" – better translated as the place of departed spirits or simply "the grave" (corresponding to the Hebrew "sheol"[2] in the Old Testament). If this is the case, the rich man wasn't in hell, but his spirit was still in torment at the thought of what lay ahead, and it was already too late to change anything.

No wonder the Bible says that *today* is the time to respond[3], and that God *now* commands all men everywhere to repent[4].

---

1 Luke 16:19-31
2 Psa 16:10
3 Heb 3:7-8
4 Acts 17:30

- Chapter 3 -

The real thing

Having pointed out that dying and going to heaven is *not* the ultimate goal for the believer (which is why the New Testament doesn't go into much detail about it), let us now consider some of the things we know about the return of Jesus – and on this topic there is no shortage of information!

It is not the purpose of this book to give a detailed exposition of the many Scriptures about this event – but I do want to present an outline of what I believe will happen. Not everyone will agree with every aspect of this (see the appendices for a discussion of some different views) – but because some readers may not be familiar with this teaching at all, I want to give you at least some idea of what we can expect, before moving on to the impact it should have on our lives today.

Look, He is coming with the clouds!

Following a time of unprecedented trouble on Earth[1], Jesus will physically return to be seen by everyone. No-one will miss it: every nation on Earth will mourn as they see Him coming on the clouds of the sky with power and great glory[2]. His appearance will light up the skies like lightning and blazing fire. He will be accompanied by a vast host of

---

1 Matt 24:21-22

2 Rev 1:7

angels, as an archangel gives a shout of command, and a trumpet sounds loudly[1].

At that time, those who have died believing in Christ will be raised with new bodies "like His glorious body"[2] and will accompany this great procession from heaven to Earth. Christians who are still alive will be "changed in the twinkling of an eye" (given new bodies without experiencing death) and caught up to meet the procession in the air[3]. The whole glorious throng will arrive on Earth, where Jesus will set up His seat of government in Jerusalem[4] (more about that in the next chapter!).

Vast multitudes will die instantly – not by any physical weapons, but just by the words that come out of Jesus' mouth and the sheer splendour of His appearance[5]. For those who don't belong to Him it will be a terrifying time of judgment which Jesus Himself compared to the flood in the days of Noah, and the fire and sulphur that rained down on Sodom – events that He said "destroyed them all"[6]. The sight of Jesus coming in such power and glory could also destroy *us* were it not that we will have new bodies – remember that even the apostle John "fell at His feet as though dead"[7] when He saw Jesus in all His splendour – but instead of this He will come "to be glorified in His holy people and to be marvelled at among all those who have believed."[8]

---

[1] Matt 24:27-31; 1 Thes 4:16; 2 Thes 1:7
[2] 1 Cor 15:51-52; Phil 3:21
[3] 1 Thes 4:17
[4] Zech 14:4-9
[5] 2 Thes 2:8; Rev 19:15-21
[6] Luke 17:26-29
[7] Rev 1:17
[8] 2 Thes 1:10

Apart from the Christians, one other group will find mercy on that day – God's ancient people the Jews. Paul wrote that Israel's heart was hardened "until the full number of the Gentiles has come in" but the day will come when "all Israel *(or 'Israel as a whole')* will be saved"[1]. We are already seeing the start of this as more Jews are turning to Christ in our generation than at any time since the days of the early church – but Gentiles are also still coming to Christ. There will come a time, however, when the door for Gentiles will be closed, but God will pour mercy on the Jewish nation. They will see the One they have pierced and the Spirit of grace will be poured upon them[2]. In that day they will say "I will praise You, O LORD; Although You were angry with me, Your anger has turned away and You have comforted me"[3].

Have you ever awaited the return of a loved one from a journey abroad? If so, you will know what it is to count down the weeks, the days and then the hours. Maybe you have even tracked their flight on the internet, alarmed by any sign of delay but excited when it gets back on schedule. Not content to wait for them to arrive at home, you have got up very early to meet them at the airport and to come back with them. Such should be our eager anticipation to welcome Jesus back to Earth, ready to leave the ground at any moment to meet Him in the air, happy that we will be reunited with all who died in Him, and content that He will now have His rightful place on Earth as King. Sadly, however, the Bible tells us that many will be asleep and unprepared for that day[4].

---

[1] Rom 11:25-26
[2] Zech 12:10
[3] Isa 12:1
[4] Matt 24:42-51

The blessed hope promised from ancient times

In his letter to Titus, Paul writes about "the blessed hope – the glorious appearing of our great God and Saviour, Jesus Christ"[1]. He doesn't say this is one of many hopes, or even our greatest hope – it is *the hope* which we eagerly await. It is important to note that "hope" in the Bible isn't used like we use it in English (meaning something that may or may not happen): the Christian hope is something we haven't experienced yet but is just as certain as things that have already happened.

This event wasn't only announced when Jesus came the first time: Jude tells us that just seven generations down from Adam, Enoch prophesied "the Lord is coming with thousands upon thousands of His holy ones to judge everyone"[2]. Job, who probably lived around the same time as Abraham, wrote about it quite specifically[3] – as did Isaiah[4], Daniel[5], Micah[6] and Zechariah[7] – and there are many other verses about the event throughout the Old Testament.

Suppose a close family member who has lived abroad for many years tells us they are coming back to live in the UK but before returning permanently, they will make a short visit to arrange their living accommodation and get other things ready. Between the two visits, we may well look back with fond memories to the first one, but we will be

---

[1] Tit 2:13

[2] Jude 14-15

[3] Job 19:25-27

[4] Isa 35:4

[5] Dan 7:13-14

[6] Mic 5:4

[7] Zech 14:3-9

looking forward with even greater eagerness to the second. Paul told us that whenever we celebrate the Lord's Supper together, we are to proclaim the Lord's death (looking back to what He did for us during His first visit) *until* He comes (looking forward to His second visit)[1] ... but so often we only look back.

A fundamental of our faith

The return of Jesus isn't a specialist subject for advanced believers – it is a fundamental doctrine of the Christian faith. We love the words of Jesus "I am going to prepare a place for you" – but He immediately continued "*if* I go and prepare a place for you, *I will come back*..."[2].

As we have already noted, the Second Coming of Jesus is prophesied many times in the Old Testament but most Jews, including Jesus' own disciples, had failed to understand He would come *twice* – hence their expectation that He would overthrow the Romans and establish His earthly kingdom during His first coming – so it is interesting to find out when Jesus Himself first mentioned that there would be a *second* coming. It was on the occasion when Simon Peter confessed "You are the Christ, the Son of the living God"[3] – undoubtedly a fundamental of our faith, but Jesus immediately taught some other important truths...

First, He stated that He would suffer, die, and rise again (and we often think about Peter's horrified reaction to the first part of this). Then Jesus says that every disciple of His *must also* deny himself and take up his cross. In other

[1] 1 Cor 11:26
[2] John 14:2-3
[3] Matt 16:16-27

words, He wouldn't immediately and dramatically establish His kingdom, but it would be a long hard road both for Him and His followers – although not forever because He concludes... "the Son of Man is *going to come* in His Father's glory...".

Following that occasion, Jesus spoke repeatedly about His death, resurrection *and* His return. Three of the gospels contain lengthy discourses about His second coming[1], and at least seven of Jesus' parables end with a day of reckoning – the weeds[2], the dragnet[3], the wedding banquet[4], the wise servant[5], the ten virgins[6], the talents[7], and the minas[8]. Jesus also spoke about the sheep and the goats, which is often referred to as a parable, but is actually a plain account of Jesus returning, and the ensuing judgment[9].

Moving on from the gospels, we find that every New Testament writer refers to this event. Paul does so many times and confirms how important it is when he writes "we believe that Jesus died and rose again" – something with which we readily agree – but goes on to say "*and so* we believe that God will bring with Jesus those who have fallen asleep in Him"[10]. In other words – if we believe the former truth, it should be a natural follow-on to believe the latter,

---

[1] Matt 24; Mk 13; Luke 21:5-36
[2] Matt 13:24-30, 36-43
[3] Matt 13:47-50
[4] Matt 22:1-14
[5] Matt 24:45-51
[6] Matt 25:1-13
[7] Matt 25:14-30
[8] Luke 19:11-27
[9] Matt 25:31-46
[10] 1 Thes 4:14

as it heralds the completion of God's purposes. The writer to the Hebrews lists six elementary teachings about Christ[1], and two of these (the resurrection of the dead and eternal judgment) relate to the Second Coming. James, whose letter is so full of practical teaching, tells his readers to be patient until the coming of the Lord our Judge[2]. Peter refers to the Lord's return in both his letters[3]. John looks forward to the day when Jesus will appear[4], Jude we have already mentioned in this chapter, and our Bibles conclude with another book from John, all about the One who "is coming with the clouds"[5].

Christians throughout the ages have included this teaching in every major creed and statement of faith – although unfortunately it is often at the end, which may be another reason why it doesn't have a more prominent place in our thinking!

The next big event on God's calendar

When I was a young Christian, I occasionally visited Church of England services, and was struck by part of their liturgy where they proclaim "Christ has died, Christ has risen, Christ will come again". At the time, it seemed a bit odd – as though these events followed in quick succession with no mention of the 2000+ year gap between the second and third events! After all, we are living in that gap so to us it's everything – but is that how God views it?

---

[1] Heb 6:1-2

[2] James 5:7-9

[3] 1 Pet 5:4; 2 Pet 3:3-14

[4] 1 John 3:2

[5] Rev 1:7

I have come to realise that from God's perspective, when Jesus returned to heaven after purchasing our salvation, His Second Coming to complete the work became the next big event on His calendar. Don't misunderstand me; I'm not saying that God hasn't been intimately involved in the last 2000 years of history – as Paul said, He determines the times and boundaries of the nations[1], and has promised to be with us as we make disciples of all nations[2] – but His eye is always on the final goal. As mentioned earlier, I fear that some Christians have become so obsessed with the *signs* of His coming, that they have lost sight of where it is all leading – but Jesus said "when these things begin to take place, stand up and lift up your heads, because *your redemption is drawing near*"[3].

There is a tendency to be critical of the Jews for not understanding that Jesus would come twice – but remember we have the benefit of hindsight! As I read Old Testament prophecies, I can understand their mistake as both comings are often mentioned in the same passage. Take, for example, Micah's prophecy about Jesus being born in Bethlehem – only two verses later he talks about Israel living securely and Jesus' greatness reaching to the ends of the Earth (although more careful study shows there is a gap in between)[4]. Again, I would suggest that God sees both comings as closely linked, with the second completing the work begun during the first. Here are two quotations from the letter to the Hebrews that bear this out:

---

[1] Acts 17:26
[2] Matt 28:18-20
[3] Luke 21:28
[4] Mic 5:2-5

"Christ was sacrificed once to take away the sins of many; and He will appear a second time, not to bear sin, but to bring salvation to those who are waiting for Him"[1].

"But when this Priest *(Jesus)* had offered for all time one sacrifice for sins, He sat down at the right hand of God. Since that time He waits for His enemies to be made His footstool"[2].

Salvation in the New Testament can refer to something we experienced in the past or is happening to us in the present – but it often relates to the future (as in the first quotation above). You may assume that the "helmet of salvation"[3] in the Christian armour refers to something we received in the past, but in another letter, Paul refers to putting on "the *hope* of salvation as a helmet"[4]. Again, we need to remember this doesn't mean something uncertain – simply that part of our salvation will be realised in the future.

The very fact that the Bible ends with Jesus saying "I am coming *soon*"[5] should tell us that on God's calendar, the day of Jesus' return is prominently highlighted, and the 2000 years in between are just like a couple of days[6].

---

[1] Heb 9:28
[2] Heb 10:12-13
[3] Eph 6:17
[4] 1 Thes 5:8
[5] Rev 22:20
[6] 2 Pet 3:8

An event that affects everyday life

Some Christians give little thought to the Second Coming on the grounds that we should concentrate on living for Christ here and now – but they fail to realise how the certainty of His return in the future has huge implications for the present.

In Peter's first letter he writes "The end of all things is near. *Therefore* be clear-minded and self-controlled so that you can pray"[1]. In his second letter, he writes in more detail about future judgment, then continues "since everything will be destroyed in this way, what kind of people ought you to be? You ought to live holy and godly lives as you look forward to the day of God... since you are looking forward to this, make every effort to be found spotless, blameless and at peace with Him"[2].

John writes about the day when Jesus will appear and we shall be like Him, but then adds "everyone who has this hope in Him purifies himself just as He is pure"[3]. In other words, if you are *really* looking forward to being like Jesus when He returns, you want to know as much as possible of that process now. Paul explains that the more we look at Jesus now, the more we become like Him[4], and John tells us that when He returns "we shall be like Him *for we shall see Him as He is*"[5] – in other words, it is the same process but speeded up. Imagine someone who is looking forward to getting married and living in wedded bliss for the rest of their life but doesn't want to spend any time with their

[1] 1 Pet 4:7
[2] 2 Pet 3:11-14
[3] 1 John 3:2-3
[4] 2 Cor 3:18
[5] 1 John 3:2

future spouse now – you would think it very strange – yet some Christians say they are looking forward to being like Jesus but don't want to know too much of the process now! The expectation of what is to come should motivate us in the present.

In his second letter to Timothy, Paul writes that his death is near but having fought a good fight, finished the race and kept the faith, he is sure there is a crown of righteousness in store for him. As we noted in Chapter 2, he doesn't expect to receive that crown when he dies and goes to heaven but says the Lord will award it to him on the day of His appearing[1]. Do you long for His appearing? Even if like Paul at that point in his life, you expect to die first, do you still long for the day when, in a new body, you will see Him as He is and be like Him?

A source of comfort

What can we say to someone whose loved one has died (assuming the loved one was a believer)?

Telling them that the deceased person is with the Lord which is far better than being here can be a great comfort, but it can also have the effect of increasing what they might already feel – that they would like to join them in heaven as soon as possible – in other words, they don't want to continue living on Earth without them. But, when our focus is on the return of Jesus, we have the hope of the deceased coming back with Him, maybe while we are still alive… "we believe that God will *bring with Jesus* those who have fallen asleep in Him"[2]. The interesting thing is

---

[1] 2 Tim 4:6-8
[2] 1 Thes 4:14

that this passage ends with the instruction "therefore encourage each other with these words"[1] – which means God has given us His own prescription for comforting the bereaved. Since I realised this, I have always written out the whole of the above passage when sending a sympathy card to the bereaved and have sometimes been told that these words have indeed been a comfort.

I well remember an elderly lady, the mother of one of our church members, visiting one Sunday morning. When speaking to her afterwards, she told me her husband had recently died, but her face lit up as she said "he believed in Jesus, so I know I will see him again...". I was fully expecting her to say "... when I die", but to my delight, she continued "when Jesus returns"! Incidentally, I then asked if she was from a Brethren background, as this is one of the few denominations to have consistently emphasised the Second Coming, and my guess was correct. Many months later (not having seen the lady in between), I planned to speak one Sunday about the Lord's return and was intending to tell this story. Nobody knew this, so imagine my joy when she turned up again that day and, when I told everybody what she had said to me, she publicly affirmed that she still had that "blessed hope" of His return.

Another group of people to whom the thought of Jesus' return is especially comforting are those being persecuted for their faith. My wife and I have been very privileged to meet many such people in different countries and they usually have a far greater awareness of the return of Jesus than we do. Paul wrote about this to the Thessalonians who as soon as they became Christians, experienced great persecution: "God is just: He will pay back trouble to those

---

[1] 1 Thes 4:18

who trouble you and give relief to you who are troubled, and to us as well. This will happen when the Lord Jesus is revealed from heaven in blazing fire with His powerful angels"[1].

God's last word to us

God's last word to us at the end of the last book in the New Testament is from the lips of Jesus Himself: "Yes, I am coming soon". There are many other important promises and warnings in Revelation 22, but they are all given in the light of this statement which appears three times: "I am coming soon"[2].

This thought was so prominent in the minds of the early Christians that they used to greet one another with the Aramaic phrase "Maranatha" (which Paul used at the end of one of his letters[3]) – it means "The Lord is coming" (or possibly "Come, O Lord"). The Jews have a wonderful greeting "Shalom", which means "peace", but "Maranatha" reminds us that the Prince of Peace will one day bring peace on Earth, as we will see in the next chapter. I know a few Christians who use this greeting and I find it a great encouragement… so much better than "Hi"!

---

1 2 Thes 1:6-7

2 Rev 22:7, 12, 20

3 1 Cor 16:22

- Chapter 4 -

The Lord will have His day

We are all familiar with expressions such as "that pop star has had his day" or "this is the day of mass communication" – but how wonderful it is to discover that *the Lord* will have *His* day…!

Isaiah, for example, said "the LORD Almighty has a *day* in store for all the proud and lofty, for all that is exalted (and they will be humbled) … the LORD alone will be exalted in *that day*"[1]. Zechariah said "a *day of the LORD* is coming… the LORD will be King over the whole Earth. On *that day* there will be one LORD, and His name the only name"[2].

The phrase "day of the Lord" is used many times in both Old and New Testaments – but what does it mean?

A 24-hour day?

Is the "day of the Lord" a 24-hour day, or is it an era like "the day of the horse and cart"? We know Jesus will return on a specific day and hour known only to His Father[3], but what about the day we read about above when the Lord alone will be exalted, and He will be King over the whole Earth – will it only last 24 hours (or maybe less) before the Earth is burned up and we go to heaven? That is what many Christians believe.

---

[1] Isa 2:12-17

[2] Zech 14:1-9

[3] Matt 24:36

As mentioned in this book's introduction, when I first started studying this topic the Lord told me not to read any books except the Bible and, although I had heard people teach about the Second Coming, it was only in general terms rather than detailed expositions – so I just started reading from Genesis to Revelation to see what it said. Something that soon became clear to me was that Jesus would one day reign on this Earth – I didn't get this from just a few verses that might have a "spiritual" interpretation, but also from many long and detailed passages (some of which we will see later in this chapter).

When I came to the New Testament, I found Jesus teaching that the meek will inherit *the Earth*[1], and teaching us to pray "Your kingdom come, Your will be done *on Earth* as it is in heaven"[2]. After His resurrection, the disciples asked Jesus "are You at this time going to restore the kingdom to Israel?" and, rather than telling them they were on the wrong track (as He often did), He replied "It is not for you to know the times or dates the Father has set by His own authority"[3].

Finally, I came to the Book of Revelation and read a passage about Christ and His people reigning on Earth for 1000 years[4] – the previous chapter having described His return, and the chapter following it describing a new heaven and a new Earth after the former ones had passed away. Actually, to be honest, I was probably aware of the "1000 year" passage before then, but I am certain I had never heard of "pre-millennialism" (the teaching that Jesus will return prior to a 1000-year reign on Earth) and I'm not sure I even knew the word "millennium" – this was long

---

[1] Matt 5:5

[2] Matt 6:10

[3] Acts 1:6-7

[4] Rev 20:1-9

before 1999 when the word became part of everyone's vocabulary and the "Millennium Dome" was built in London. I certainly hadn't heard anyone teach about this, and well remember going to a famous preacher I knew and very tentatively telling him I had come to believe Jesus would reign on Earth for 1000 years – and being very relieved when he told me he also believed that!

... or a 1000-year day?

The passage in Revelation actually mentions "1000 years" *six times*. Although, as I said, I believe this earthly reign of Christ is mentioned many times in the Bible, it seems God left it until the end of the book to tell us the length – but then made sure there was no doubt about it!

There is, however, a clue in Peter's second letter when he writes about the Second Coming of Jesus, the *day* of judgment and destruction of the ungodly, and the *day* of the Lord – and in the middle of this passage says "with the Lord a *day* is like a thousand years, and a thousand years are like a *day*"[1]. You may object that Peter is simply stating that God's timing is different to ours when it comes to the promise of Christ's return – and in some ways I agree with you – but find it interesting that a "1000-year day" is mentioned in this particular context.

I am utterly convinced that the last 1000 years of Earth's history will be the "Lord's day" in the fullest sense of that phrase. You may have heard people in a church service quoting John's words "on the Lord's Day I was in the Spirit"[2] and praying that we too would be in the Spirit this

---

[1] 2 Pet 3:7-10
[2] Rev 1:10

Sunday, but I am not at all convinced John received his revelation on a Sunday. There is nowhere else in the New Testament where Sunday is called the "Lord's day" but, in the Roman Empire, the phrase "Lord's day" referred to a day when they celebrated their belief that "Caesar is lord". John was on the isle of Patmos because he believed and proclaimed that "Jesus is Lord" – so could it be that he received his revelation on the day of the Roman celebration and/or was taken in the Spirit to that "day" at the end of history when everything said and done will proclaim the Lordship of Jesus Christ?

As some will know, "pre-millennialism" (the conviction I hold) is not the only view. There is "post-millennialism" (Jesus will return *after* the 1000-year period), amillennialism (there is *no* literal 1000-year period) and "pan-millennialism" (a humorous term meaning we don't know and don't care very much, but it will all pan out in the end) – but there will be no more technical terms like these in this chapter and we will just use "the Millennium" to refer to Jesus' 1000-year reign on Earth after He returns. I don't intend to argue the case for this but will simply present what I read in the Scriptures and hope you will become as thrilled as I am with this wonderful aspect of God's plan.

Who will be there?

Who will be on Earth during the Millennium? The passage in Revelation specifically mentions those who were martyred for their faith[1], but this is only an example given to highlight the complete turnaround: those once killed by evil authorities are now part of the government! Before that,

---

1 Rev 20:4

however, it mentions “thrones on which were seated those who had been given authority to judge” and earlier in the book we read “... with Your blood You purchased men for God from every tribe and language and people and nation. You have made them to be a kingdom and priests to serve our God, and they *will reign on the Earth*”[1] – so this sounds like all Christians will be there and is confirmed by statements about the Lord coming with *all* His saints[2]. On the other hand, Jesus promised to those *who overcome and do His will to the end* “I will give authority over the nations”[3] – but can someone who doesn’t fit this description really be called a Christian? Read on...

Christians will be there in resurrection bodies they will receive when Jesus returns to Earth (whether or not they were alive at the time) and will no longer be subject to disease or death. Also present, however, will be some unbelievers who were alive at the time of His return, and will continue to reproduce and to die[4]. The rest of the dead (i.e. unbelievers who died throughout history), we are told, will not come to life until the 1000 years are ended[5].

If you are wondering if there will be enough room on Earth for all these people, bear in mind that the population of unbelievers will be greatly reduced by judgments on the Earth before and after Jesus returns, and that large uninhabitable areas will be transformed (more about both of these later). Maybe the most challenging explanation, however, is found in what Jesus Himself said: “Not everyone who says to Me, ‘Lord, Lord,’ will enter the

---

1 Rev 5:9-10
2 Zech 14:5; 1 Thes 3:13
3 Rev 2:26
4 Isa 65:20; Zech 8:3-5
5 Rev 20:5

kingdom of heaven, but only he who does the will of My Father who is in heaven. *Many* will say to Me on that day, 'Lord, Lord, did we not prophesy in Your name, and in Your name drive out demons, and perform many miracles?' Then I will tell them plainly, 'I never knew you. Away from Me, you evildoers!'"[1].

A day when deception is removed

In the passage in Revelation about the Millennium, it states that Satan will be thrown into the abyss that will be locked and sealed "to keep him from *deceiving* the nations anymore until the 1000 years were ended"[2].

The chief work of Satan from the Garden of Eden onwards has been to deceive, and he even masquerades as an angel of light[3]. That's why the people around us have so many erroneous views about God, and why there are so many false religions and cults. Many people are very sincere in their beliefs but are sincerely wrong, and it is only the gospel of Jesus Christ that can "open their eyes and turn them from darkness to light, and from the power of Satan to God"[4]. There will, however, come a day (the 1000-year day) when that deception will be removed and everyone on Earth will see the truth – as Zechariah said "the LORD will be King over the whole Earth. On that day there will be one LORD, and His name the only name"[5]. Isaiah said "the LORD alone will be exalted in that day"[6] and

---

[1] Matt 7:21-23
[2] Rev 20:3
[3] 2 Cor 11:14
[4] Acts 26:18
[5] Zech 14:9
[6] Isa 2:17

"the Earth will be full of the knowledge of the LORD"[1]. In other words, people will no longer say that Allah is God, or that we need the writings of Joseph Smith or Mary Baker Eddy to understand the truth – all these names will disappear, and the name of the Lord will be the only one that holds sway. That name is Jesus.

This doesn't mean everyone on Earth will obey Jesus (after the words above, Zechariah goes on to speak about those who will not worship the King[2]) but nobody will be in any doubt about who the rightful King is. No-one will be able to say they didn't know the truth, so rebellion in the human heart rather than deception, will be exposed as the real problem.

A day when justice is established

Has anyone ever asked you why God doesn't sort out all the injustice in the world? Why doesn't He stop the rich oppressing the poor? Why doesn't He end all the bloodshed? Maybe you replied that God has given man a free choice so these things aren't God's fault or maybe you explained there is an enemy called Satan and mankind is under his control – but there is a much simpler answer "*He will*".

Jesus *will* establish justice on Earth when He returns and do all those things people think He should do – but it won't be to everyone's taste! The Bible says He will rule the nations with an iron sceptre[3], but it also says He will make

[1] Isa 11:9
[2] Zech 14:17-19
[3] Psa 2:9

just decisions for the poor and needy[1]. Unlike many rulers who start with these good intentions but fail to see them through, He will "not falter or be discouraged till He establishes justice on Earth"[2].

When Jesus entered Jerusalem during His earthly ministry, He rode on a young donkey[3] symbolising the fact that He wasn't coming as a military leader – but Revelation gives us a very different picture of His Second Coming. This time He is seen riding on a horse and *making war*, and the armies of heaven that follow Him (resurrected believers) are also riding horses. Out of His mouth comes a sharp sword with which to strike down the nations that He will rule with an iron sceptre, and He treads the winepress of *the fury of the wrath of God Almighty*. If that isn't terrifying enough, we then read about a feast for the birds – the flesh of kings, generals, mighty men ... and all people, small and great[4]. This is slaughter on a massive scale, but we cannot expect God to be patient forever – the day of His wrath will come[5].

After this initial "battle", however, from which Jesus and His followers emerge totally victorious, the Millennium will mainly be a time of peace on Earth[6]. Solomon's reign was, in many ways, a picture of this era. Nathan prophesied about Solomon "I will be his Father, and he will be My son"[7] but when that verse is quoted in the New Testament, the writer applies it to God and His Son Jesus[8]. It often happens in Scripture that one prophecy has several

---

[1] Isa 11:4
[2] Isa 42:4
[3] Luke 19:35
[4] Rev 19:11-17
[5] Rev 6:15-17
[6] Isa 9:7
[7] 2 Sam 7:14
[8] Heb 1:5

fulfilments, with the former ones being pictures of the ultimate and greatest fulfilment – and so it is with Solomon. Unlike David, whose reign was marked by bloodshed, Solomon's reign was a time of peace. The nation of Israel occupied more of the territory God had promised them than at any other time, and people came from afar to hear the wisdom of Solomon (although we know he had serious flaws and his power, though great, was limited). When he came to the throne, his father David wrote Psalm 72 as a prayer for Solomon but again, it seems to speak of Someone, and something much greater. I encourage you to read the whole Psalm yourself, but here are a few tasters…

> "He will defend the afflicted among the people and save the children of the needy; he will crush the oppressor… In his days the righteous will flourish; prosperity will abound till the moon is no more. He will rule from sea to sea and from the River to the ends of the Earth… All kings will bow down to him and all nations will serve him. For he will deliver the needy who cry out, the afflicted who have no one to help. He will take pity on the weak and the needy and save the needy from death. He will rescue them from oppression and violence, for precious is their blood in His sight."[1]

Solomon only fulfilled a fraction of that but one day Jesus will fulfil it all – and in case you aren't convinced that Psalm 72 is about Jesus, here is something Isaiah wrote specifically about Him:

---

[1] Psa 72:4-14

"He will not judge by what He sees with His eyes or decide by what He hears with His ears; but with righteousness He will judge *(in favour of)* the needy, with justice He will give decisions for the poor of the Earth. He will strike the Earth with the rod of His mouth; with the breath of His lips He will slay the wicked. Righteousness will be His belt and faithfulness the sash around His waist."[1]

A day when the curse starts to be reversed

Another question often raised by unbelievers (and sometimes believers) is why God allows disasters and suffering that are completely outside man's control. Why are some areas of the world smitten by climatic conditions and pestilences that make it hard for the inhabitants to survive? Why do lions kill lambs? Why are some people disabled and some die prematurely?

All these, of course, are results of the "curse" (or curses) that God pronounced after the first man and woman sinned[2], but will they only be removed in heaven? We don't read of any trees, fields or animals in heaven, yet Isaiah spoke of a day when "the wolf will live with the lamb, the leopard will lie down with the goat, the calf and the lion and the yearling together; and a little child will lead them. The cow will feed with the bear, their young will lie down together, and the lion will eat straw like the ox. The infant will play near the cobra's den, and the young child will put its hand into the viper's nest". Many assume this is figurative language and apply it to heaven, but the passage

---

[1] Isa 11:3-5

[2] Gen 3:14-19

concludes "… for the *Earth* will be filled with the knowledge of the LORD as the waters cover the sea"[1].

The same prophet also said "The desert and the parched land will be glad; the wilderness will rejoice and blossom. Like the crocus, it will burst into bloom; it will rejoice greatly and shout for joy. The glory of Lebanon will be given to it, the splendour of Carmel and Sharon… Then will the eyes of the blind be opened and the ears of the deaf unstopped. Then will the lame leap like a deer, and the mute tongue shout for joy. Water will gush forth in the wilderness and streams in the desert. The burning sand will become a pool, the thirsty ground bubbling springs. In the haunts where jackals once lay, grass and reeds and papyrus will grow"[2].

In the Millenium, we will see God's original magnificent creation restored, but it would not be true to say that the curse will be completely removed. We noted earlier that unbelievers will still be in their natural bodies and subject to death, and those who refuse to submit to the rule of Jesus will suffer drought and plagues[3] – but we also read about Jerusalem "never again will there be in it an infant who lives but a few days, or an old man who does not live out his years; the one who dies at 100 will be thought a mere youth; he who fails to reach 100 will be considered accursed"[4] …and… "once again men and women of ripe old age will sit in the streets of Jerusalem, each of them with cane in hand because of their age. The city streets will be filled with boys and girls playing there"[5].

---

[1] Isa 11:6-9

[2] Isa 35:1-7

[3] Zech 14:12-19

[4] Isa 65:20

[5] Zech 8:3-5

Not everything changed instantly when Adam and Eve were expelled from Eden: we read about people living many hundreds of years[1] until after the Flood, then lifespans gradually reduced to a maximum of 120[2]. It also appears that people were vegetarians (and maybe lived at peace with the animals) until Noah came out of the ark[3] – but before long, the fall of man affected the whole of creation. Similarly, not everything will become like the Garden of Eden during the Millenium, but things will start to move in that direction until (as we shall see in the next chapter) the curse is completely removed.

A day of rest

On the seventh day of creation God rested. "Rest" in the Bible doesn't necessarily denote complete inactivity but a state of contentment because something has been achieved – so, having seen that everything He had made was very good, God rested on the seventh day.[4]

That contentment, however, didn't last long, and soon we read that God's heart was filled with pain at man's wickedness, so He decided to wipe out all mankind except Noah (whose name means "rest") and his family[5]. For six months the Earth was flooded with water: the first time Noah sent out a dove, it found no place of rest[6], but eventually the waters subsided, everyone came out of the ark, and Noah offered sacrifices to the Lord, who smelled

---

1 Gen 5

2 Gen 6:3

3 Gen 9:3

4 Gen 1:31 - 2:2

5 Gen 6:6-8

6 Gen 8:9

the "pleasing" or "soothing" aroma[1]. Again, something had been achieved and, after the turmoil of the Flood, the Earth was at rest (albeit for a brief period).

When Jesus returns, He will again judge the Earth and, as we have said, there will be unprecedented slaughter and destruction – but that's not the end of the story for this planet (as some would have us believe). Yes, it will eventually be destroyed by fire[2], but before then, Isaiah states "He will judge between the nations and will settle disputes for many peoples. They will beat their swords into ploughshares *(farming implements)* and their spears into pruning hooks *(ditto)*. Nation will not take up sword against nation, nor will they train for war anymore"[3]. Micah says something very similar but adds "every man will sit under his own vine and under his own fig tree, and no one will make them afraid"[4]. What a picture of rest and contentment! Isaiah also says in that day Jesus will "stand as a Banner for the peoples; the nations will rally to Him, and His *place of rest* will be glorious"[5].

Finally, Isaiah also wrote "He who fashioned and made the Earth... did not create it to be empty but formed it to be inhabited"[6]. If God simply judged and destroyed this world, it could seem that His purposes had failed, but that *isn't* what will happen – *the last day will be His*. Just as God's first work on Earth ended with a day of rest, so will the history of this world.

---

[1] Gen 8:21
[2] 2 Pet 3:7
[3] Isa 2:4
[4] Mic 4:3-4
[5] Isa 11:10
[6] Isa 45:18

A day when God fulfils His promises to Israel

This section deserves a book of its own – and many such books have already been written, but I just want to emphasise what Paul wrote to the Romans about the Israelites "did God reject His people? *By no means!*"[1]. We already saw in Chapter 3 that, when Jesus returns, the nation of Israel as a whole will recognise their Messiah but, following that, they will have an important role in the Millenium.

Just as Paul wrote about Israel being hardened "*until* the full number of the Gentiles has come in"[2], so Micah also uses the word "until" in his famous prophecy about Jesus being born in Bethlehem that we mentioned in Chapter 2. He says "Israel will be abandoned *until* the time when she who is in labour gives birth and the rest of His brothers return to join the Israelites" and after that "they will live securely, for then His greatness will reach to the ends of the Earth and He will be their peace"[3].

Ezekiel's famous prophecy about the valley of dry bones is frequently applied to the church, yet it clearly states "these bones are the whole house of Israel"[4]. The prophecy then speaks of a time when Israel will return to their own land, and "all the nations will know that I the LORD make Israel holy"[5]. The first part has been fulfilled from 1948 onwards, but the remainder is yet to happen.

---

[1] Rom 11:1
[2] Rom 11:25
[3] Mic 5:2-5
[4] Ezek 37:11
[5] Ezek 37:21-28

Zechariah said God will pour out His grace on His people and "they will look on Me, the One they have pierced"[1]. He also said that people from many nations will come to Jerusalem to seek the Lord and "in those days ten men from all languages and nations will take firm hold of one Jew by the hem of his robe and say 'Let us go with you, because we have heard that God is with you'"[2]. What a reversal of the persecution and rejection that Jews have experienced throughout history!

So, we could continue quoting many other similar statements by the Old Testament prophets. Although some of these prophecies have been partially fulfilled in Israel's history, there clearly hasn't been a complete fulfilment, and this leaves us with two options: either we give "spiritual" meanings to the prophecies and say they have been fulfilled in the church instead of the nation of Israel (which may be feasible in some cases, but still leaves a lot unexplained) – or we accept that a literal fulfilment is yet future. The millenial reign of Israel's Messiah in Jerusalem provides a perfect explanation.

A day when the saints reign on Earth with Jesus

In the book of Daniel, he describes a dream in which he saw "one like a Son of Man coming with the clouds of heaven... He was given authority, glory and sovereign power; all peoples, nations, and men of every language worshipped Him"[3] – yet later he writes "the sovereignty, power and greatness of the kingdoms under the whole

---

[1] Zech 12:10

[2] Zech 8:20-23

[3] Dan 7:13-14

heaven will be handed over to *the saints*, the people of the Most High"[1].

Jesus Himself, in His message to the church in Thyatira, says "To him who overcomes and does My will to the end, I will give authority over the nations" and then goes on to apply a passage in the Psalms to His people[2] although the primary application is clearly to Himself[3].

Not only is Jesus returning to reign on Earth, but *His people* will reign with Him. It can be dangerous to establish doctrines from parables, but it is interesting to note that in three of these illustrations Jesus gave, the faithful servants are given positions of responsibility when He returns. In one, they are put in charge of 5 or 10 cities[4]. In another they are put in charge of all the Master's possessions[5] and, in the third, put in charge of many things[6].

It also appears that believers will have a role in judging Israel and the Gentile nations. Jesus said to His disciples "when the Son of Man sits on His glorious throne, you who have followed Me will also sit on twelve thrones, judging the twelve tribes of Israel"[7]. Paul wrote to the Corinthians "do you not know that the saints will judge the world?"[8] – and John in Revelation "saw thrones on which were seated those who had been given authority to judge"[9].

---

[1] Dan 7:27
[2] Rev 2:26-27
[3] Psa 2:7-9
[4] Luke 19:11-27
[5] Matt 24:47
[6] Matt 25:19-23
[7] Matt 19:28
[8] 1 Cor 6:2
[9] Rev 20:4

Actually, God always intended mankind to rule the Earth under His authority. When He first made man, He said "let them *rule over* the fish of the sea and the birds of the air, over the livestock, over all the Earth, and over all the creatures that move along the ground"[1], but Adam and Eve failed at the first hurdle and couldn't even rule over a snake! The truth is that when we act independently of the Lord, we have no authority at all but, when we submit to the authority of Christ, we reign with Him.

A day with an unexpected ending

The passage in Revelation about the 1000 years has a *very* unexpected ending: "When the 1000 years are over, Satan will be released from his prison and will go out to deceive the nations in the four corners of the Earth... and to gather them for battle. In number they are like the sand on the seashore. They marched across the breadth of the Earth and surrounded the camp of God's people, the city He loves. But fire came down from heaven and devoured them."[2]

How can it be that after 1000 years of peace on Earth, with all the blessings described earlier in this chapter, Satan is able to assemble an army to try to overthrow the kingdom of God? One answer is that he will use the same tactic he has been using from the Garden of Eden onwards but was unable to use for 1000 years – he will go out to *deceive* the nations – but another answer is that this *will prove God is right*. So often men and women have said that if only the conditions were right, we could make a perfect world. If only there was no poverty, no disease, no disasters. If only

---

[1] Gen 1:26

[2] Rev 20:7-9

the government wasn't corrupt. If only, if only ... but all this ignores the fact that the problem lies within each of us – our sinful nature is in rebellion against God. This surprise ending to the Millenium proves what the Bible has always said about us, and God's final judgment on unrepentant sinners is perfectly just.

How does all this affect us here and now?

Personally, I have found the teaching about the Millennium makes a big difference to my life here and now. I find it hard to imagine what heaven is like, but much easier to visualise the planet where I currently live being ruled by Jesus and His people.

I think this first came home to me when my wife and I were in Calcutta, one of the most polluted cities on Earth. Unless you've been there, it's hard to imagine just what it is like: as we walked along the streets, we were constantly watching where we were treading and were very reluctant to buy any food or drink, even if it was packaged. There are some wonderful Christian works in that city – hospitals and feeding programs – but the problems are so vast that it is hard to imagine how Calcutta could ever be cleaned up. What government or charity could ever do it? How could they change the way people have lived for generations...? But it *will* happen when Jesus returns! This doesn't mean there is no point in trying to do anything now – quite the reverse – and any work that is started now in the name of Christ will be completed when He returns.

At the other extreme, I've stood on mountain tops admiring the incredible works of God's creation and thought to myself that if it's so wonderful *now*, what will it be when the desert blossoms like a rose. When people ask me if there will be animals in heaven, I reply probably not, because heaven is a place for spirits rather than bodies... but I tell them there will *definitely* be animals on Earth when Jesus returns to reign – and they won't be eating or attacking each other!

Christians are called to be the salt and light of the Earth – helping to stop the rot spreading and influencing society for good. Again, knowing that Jesus has plans for this Earth increases my inspiration to do this work. I won't reap the rewards in heaven if I die, but on this Earth. I'm not expecting to be put in charge of Great Britain, but maybe I will have a place in the local council – so why not start working for the good of my neighbourhood now?

We mentioned earlier Paul's statement that the saints will judge the world, and he draws a very practical conclusion from this – that we should be competent to judge issues in the church now, and even says that men of little account in the church should be able to do this[1]! *Every* Christian should be learning to exercise discernment and to give wise counsel to others, whereas so often we leave it all to "the pastor".

Finally, I'm not *so* concerned about whether I meet my family and friends in heaven as I have such limited understanding of what heaven will be like – but I would like them, and all my readers, to be on this Earth during the Millennium. Maybe we will be alive when Jesus returns but, if we don't belong to Him, we will still die at some point (maybe very soon as He executes His judgments on Earth). The only sure way of being here throughout those 1000 years is to be His disciple now and remain faithful until the end.

---

[1] 1 Cor 6:1-4

- *Chapter 5* -

A new heaven and a new Earth

I hope I have convinced you (or at least made you consider) that the final era of history on this Earth will be a glorious demonstration of what life can be like when Jesus is in charge – but what will happen *after that*? Will we finally go to heaven and live there forever?

First, the Bible tells us, planet Earth and the entire planetary system will disappear. Peter says they will be burned up with intense heat[1], whereas John simply says they will "flee away" with no more place for them as God's judgment throne is revealed[2]. At this point, *all the unrighteous dead* will be raised[3], mankind will be judged and "if anyone's name was not found written in the book of life, he was thrown into the lake of fire"[4]. So will we now go to heaven? No! ... and we never will (unless we die before Jesus returns) because, as John goes on to say "I saw a new heaven *and a new Earth*"[5] – and Peter says *this* is what we are ultimately looking forward to.[6]

---

[1] 2 Pet 3:7, 10, 12
[2] Rev 20:11
[3] Rev 20:5, 12-13
[4] Rev 20:15
[5] Rev 21:1
[6] 2 Pet 3:13

Our Father on Earth

John makes it clear that our destination isn't heaven where God lives now, or even a new heaven, but a *new Earth* where *God will live with His people*. God and Jesus will have their throne in the Holy City – the new Jerusalem – which will *come down* from heaven to the new Earth[1].

When God created our present Earth, His dwelling place remained in heaven, but He walked in the Garden of Eden in the cool of the day (and maybe at other times), seeking fellowship with the man and woman He had made[2]. Again and again throughout history we see that God has reached out to the human race – but now we read that He will change His address and *live* with them! To be invited to God's home in heaven is wonderful, but for God to come to live with us is even more amazing, and surely the ultimate wonder. God the Son already lived here for 33 years while His Father remained in heaven – and this will happen again in the Millennium – but ultimately *both Father and Son* will make the new Earth Their permanent address.

A new creation

The new Earth will contain all the wonders of creation that, even in this fallen world, declare God's glory – rivers, mountains, trees, fruit, gold and precious stones are all mentioned in John's vision. I haven't found any mention of animals in the new Earth but, since God brought them to Adam in the garden of Eden, and since they will be present in the Millennium, I have no doubt they will also be in the

---

1 Rev 21:1-3

2 Gen 3:8

new Earth. (A reference to the dogs being outside[1] is a description of the morally depraved as used elsewhere in Scripture[2]!)

Something that will be absent is the sea[3], which has often been associated with peril or tumult[4], and it also separates nations. There will, it seems, still be nations[5] – but now there will be no division, and we are told that the leaves of the tree of life are "for the healing of the nations"[6]. Also gone is the night and, although we are not specifically told there will be no sun, it certainly isn't needed in the new Jerusalem because "the glory of God gives it light, and the Lamb is its lamp"[7].

Not everything about the new Earth is easy to understand. The Holy City, for example, is described as a cube (1400 miles long by 1400 miles wide by 1400 miles high)[8] – is it a multi-storey structure? And who lives outside (albeit with the ability to come in at any time)[9]? I also used to wonder who will be in the new heaven, since God will be living on Earth, but this could simply refer to the skies and the planets which, I am sure, He will also re-create in all their splendour.

The fact is that the Bible does not give us so much information about the new Earth as it does about the Millennium (hence this chapter will be a lot shorter than the

---

1 Rev 22:15
2 Deut 23:18; 2 Pet 2:22
3 Rev 21:1
4 Psa 46:2-3; Lukę 21:25
5 Rev 21:24,26
6 Rev 22:2
7 Rev 21:23
8 Rev 21:16
9 Rev 21:24-26

previous one) – and I believe that's deliberate. Even Isaiah, after announcing that God will create new heavens and a new Earth, quickly shifts his focus to the Millennium[1]. The reign of Jesus on Earth is the next phase of history after His return, so it should also be our immediate focus. Maybe, during that era, Jesus will teach us more about the new Earth and prepare us for it – but we will just have to wait and see!

A new order

One thing Peter does tell us about the new Earth is that it is the "home of righteousness"[2]. We have already thought about the prayer "Your Kingdom come, Your will be done *on Earth* as it is in heaven" being answered during the Millennium but, even in that era, death will still be present[3] and there will still be some effects of the curse[4]. In other words, there will be plenty of reminders of what the Earth was like before Jesus returned – but in the new Earth "there will be no more death or mourning or crying or pain, for the *old order of things has passed away*"[5] and "no longer will there be *any curse*"[6].

One of the most striking examples of the new order is that there will be no temple in the Holy City because God the Father and Jesus are its Temple[7]. There is no literal temple on Earth now of course, but both the church and our

---

1 Isa 65:17-20
2 2 Pet 3:13
3 Isa 65:20
4 Zech 14:12-19
5 Rev 21:4
6 Rev 22:3
7 Rev 21:22

bodies are figuratively described as such – and the Bible tells us that God dwells in both of these *by His Spirit*[1]. We see and feel the effect of the Holy Spirit, but we don't see *Him* and our experience is limited – hence Paul says "now we see but a poor reflection in a mirror" but continues "then we shall see face to face"[2].

Unlike the Millennium, the new Earth isn't God demonstrating how He can put things right in the old order but creating a *completely new order*. Isaiah says "the former things will not be remembered, nor will they come to mind"[3], which is why it is so difficult for us to grasp it now. Indeed, Paul says that what God has prepared for us cannot be conceived with the eye, ear or mind – in other words anything we read or write about it are just glimpses – but he goes on to say it has been revealed to us by His Spirit[4]. The Holy Spirit within us is the "deposit guaranteeing our inheritance until the redemption of those who are God's possession"[5]. Hallelujah!

---

[1] Eph 2:21-22; 1 Cor 6:19
[2] 1 Cor 13:9-12
[3] Isa 65:17
[4] 1 Cor 2:9-10
[5] Eph 1:14

- *Chapter 6* -
What kind of people should we be?

In chapter 3, we quoted from Peter's second letter where, having spoken about the day of the Lord and the complete destruction of our entire planetary system, he asks "Since everything will be destroyed in this way, *what kind of people ought you to be*?"[1]. As we near the end of this book, it would be good for us to consider our answer to that very important question in greater detail.

Whether or not you agree with every point I have made, I hope and pray you are at least thinking more about the return of Jesus than you were previously. Maybe you have realised what a neglected topic it is, and maybe you have learned some things you didn't know before – but where will you go from here? This chapter contains a few practical suggestions.

Stop saying nothing

In the second book of Samuel, we read about a rebellion against David, God's anointed king of Israel[2]. His son Absalom started spreading the lie that he would be a better king and stole the hearts of the people, so David and some loyal followers had to leave Jerusalem until Absalom died in battle – but, even then, there was no rush to re-instate

---

1 2 Pet 3:11
2 2 Sam 15ff

David. Throughout Israel, we read, people were arguing with each other saying "The king delivered us from the hand of our enemies; he is the one who rescued us from the hand of the Philistines. But now he has fled the country because of Absalom; and Absalom, whom we anointed to rule over us, has died in battle. *So why do you say nothing about bringing the king back?*"[1].

It is by no means a perfect illustration, but this story does contain some pointers to the situation in which we find ourselves today. The Lord Jesus Christ is God's chosen King but, except by a few, He has been rejected. His enemy the devil has convinced the world he would be a better king, but his lies have been exposed and the world is getting worse and worse. Yet, it seems, most followers of Jesus are in no hurry for Him to return and to claim the earthly kingdom which is rightfully His – instead of that, we are arguing with each other! Why do we say nothing about bringing *our* King back?

We may not know what to say, or how to say it, but let us at least say *something*! Preachers, teachers, and anyone taking a leading role in Christian meetings need to set an example, so I will address these people first in the next section.

Preach it

If you are a preacher or teacher, it would be worth asking yourself how often you have taught about the Second Coming of Jesus in the last year, and how that compares to

---

[1] 2 Sam 19:9-10

the frequency with which it is mentioned in the New Testament.

If you have avoided the topic because you consider it too complex or controversial, I hope this book has illustrated the fact that quite a lot can be said without entering more difficult territory – you could, for example, start with one of Jesus' parables (simple stories about everyday things) that teach about the importance of being ready for His return.

There are also specific occasions when this topic is especially relevant. If, for example, you are taking a funeral, this is an ideal opportunity to tell everyone that not only is Jesus coming back to Earth *but so also are those who die believing in Him*. Why spend all the time speaking about heaven – about which we know very little, and where departed believers live only on a temporary basis – when there is so much Biblical material about the resurrection of the dead and the age to come? If it is your custom to speak about Jesus' first coming at Christmas time, why not take the opportunity to preach about His second coming? If you are leading a communion service, do you refer only to what Jesus did in the past or do you, like Jesus at the Last Supper, look forward to a glorious future[1]? Do you just "proclaim the Lord's death" or do you remember that it is "until He comes"[2]?

If you feel prompted to preach about the Second Coming next week but don't mention it again for a year, it will convey the impression that it isn't very prominent in your thinking. Sometimes it is the "off the cuff" remarks rather than a carefully prepared message that speaks to people. When leading in prayer, for example, do you ever make any

---

[1] Matt 26:29
[2] 1 Cor 11:26

mention of His return? (We will be saying more about prayer later).

SIng it

The things we sing – both in the world and in the church – have a great influence on us.

Some Christians today find it hard to learn doctrine – and that's nothing new – but one of the ways people learned it in the past was by singing about it. On many important occasions in the Bible, songs were written to help people understand and remember what God had done. After the Israelites crossed the Red Sea for example, they sang a song to commemorate the event[1] and, just before his death, Moses taught them another song[2]. Many of the Psalms recount God's dealings with Israel[3] and were written so that future generations would learn what He has done, and understand His ways.

A song will often stick in a person's mind longer than a spoken message – so it is very important that the songs we sing in our meetings are Biblically based. In recent years the trend has been towards choruses with very limited content, which have their place but don't teach us very much. On the other hand, I looked through a Christian song book produced in the 1960s which contained only 100 songs, but they covered most of the fundamental doctrines of our faith. 30 of the songs contained some reference to our future hope – although only 11 of these specifically referred to Jesus returning. Another 14 portrayed our

---

[1] Exod 15:1-18

[2] Deut 31:30 – 32:43

[3] e.g. Psa 103 – 107

ultimate destiny as heaven and in five of the songs it was unclear where we will end up! Just two songs mentioned that Jesus is returning to reign on Earth. You may find it interesting to do a similar analysis of the songs sung in your meetings over the last three months for example.

Some of the songs we do sing that contain references to Jesus' return are actually very old but some have been set to new music – such as "My hope is built on nothing less" with the final verse "When He shall come with trumpet sound"[1], and "Living He loved me … one day He's coming oh glorious day!"[2]. Another outstanding old song is "When peace like a river", which speaks of death (signified by the river Jordan) as a *possibility* rather than a certainty: "For me, be it Christ, be it Christ hence to live: If Jordan above me shall roll …" but the next verse states our *certain* hope:

> But Lord, 'tis for Thee, for Thy coming we wait,
> The sky, not the grave, is our goal;
> Oh, trump of the angel! Oh, voice of the Lord!
> Blessed hope, blessed rest of my soul.[3]

There are a few newer songs with these themes: I think, for example, of "These are the days of Elijah" with its magnificent chorus "Behold He comes riding on the clouds"[4]. Then there is "Blessing and honour glory and power"[5] which paraphrases the words of Daniel with "Your kingdom shall reign over all the Earth"[6] … and I think of the final verse of "I cast my mind to Calvary":

---

1 E.Mote (1834)
2 J.W.Chapman (1859-1918)
3 H.G.Spafford (1873)
4 R.Mark (1994)
5 G.Sadler & J.Harvill (1992)
6 Dan 7:14

He shall return in robes of white
The blazing sun shall pierce the night
And I will rise among the saints
My gaze transfixed on Jesus' face.[1]

Maybe you can think of others – if so, how about singing them more often? Or, if you are a songwriter, perhaps you could help to bring these wonderful truths to the forefront of our thinking again?

Talk about it

Even if you are not a public speaker, worship leader or songwriter – you can still bring the topic of the Lord's return into your everyday conversation (like the elderly lady I mentioned in Chapter 3). We can encourage each other (especially those mourning the loss of a loved one) with these words "the Lord Himself will come down from heaven…"[2] – or greet each other with "Marantha *(the Lord is coming)*!"[3].

When speaking with unbelievers, someone may say "I don't know what the world is coming to" – which is an ideal opportunity to tell them Who is coming to the world! You may even be able to mention Bible prophecies that are being fulfilled, such as Jerusalem being the constant centre of attention[4]. Others may quote the words of Benjamin Franklin "the only certainties in life are death and taxes" – but you can reply that the first of these isn't true – actually, the Christian has *many* certainties and one of them is that

---

[1] M.W.Sampson & B.W.Hastings & D.M.Ussher (2015)
[2] 1 Thes 4:16-18
[3] 1 Cor 16:22
[4] Zech 12:1-3

Jesus will return to Earth and, if that happens in our lifetime, *we will never die*. What a talking point!

Pray it

Let's remind ourselves again how the New Testament ends: the Spirit and the bride *(the church)* say "Come!". Jesus responds "Yes, I am coming soon", and John adds his own prayer "Amen. Come Lord Jesus"[1]. I wonder if we have ever prayed "Come Lord Jesus"?

Some may think this is a pointless prayer, since the Bible makes it clear that God has already fixed the date[2] – but how did He do this? Was it an arbitrary choice, or was it based on His foreknowledge of what would be happening on the Earth? And if the latter, can we have any influence on that? According to most English translations, Peter tells us to "look forward to the day of God and *speed its coming*"[3] – implying that we *can* influence the date (although some translate the last phrase "wait eagerly for it to come"). In his revelation, John sees an angel offering a bowl of incense on the altar before God's throne; the smoke of the incense *together with the prayers of the saints* goes up to God, then the same bowl is filled with fire and hurled on the Earth resulting in a series of judgments leading up to the return of Christ[4]. Could this mean that our prayers have an influence on the timetable for end time events?

---

1 Rev 22:17,20

2 Matt 24:36; Acts 1:7

3 2 Pet 3:12

4 Rev 8:4-5

Ultimately I don't know the answers to these questions, but what I am sure about is that we shouldn't be passively sitting back as if we don't really care when our King is coming. If someone you love is away from home you will urge them to return as quickly as possible, even if you know it won't happen for some time. You will tell them you can't wait to see them again and share your excitement with others. It is interesting to note that when God's Spirit moves in power, people often wake up to the fact that Jesus will return. It is said that before the Welsh revival of 1904, hardly anyone was preaching about the Second Coming, but following the revival, it became a favourite topic. Similarly, the early Pentecostals were nicknamed "the Second Comers" because they placed so much emphasis on this doctrine.

Many have missed the fact that in Jesus' parable about five foolish and five wise virgins[1], *all ten* fell asleep because the bridegroom was a long time coming – then a cry rang out that He was on the way, and five got ready to meet Him. We can find that cry loud and clear throughout the New Testament. God's Spirit has reinforced it, especially in times of revival – and this little book is my effort to cry out. May God give us grace to listen and respond.

Live it

Let us now return to the quotation with which we started this chapter, and see how Peter answered his own question: "Since everything will be destroyed in this way, what kind of people ought you to be? You ought to live holy and godly lives as you look forward to the day of God and

---

[1] Matt 25:1-13

speed its coming ... make every effort to be found spotless, blameless and at peace with Him."[1]

The most important response to these truths about the future is to live exemplary lives now, and to be at peace with God. We have already thought in Chapter 3 about the fact that if we are *really* looking forward to being made like Jesus, we will want as much as possible of that experience now.

It can be very easy, when presented with the glorious truths of His return, to re-dedicate our lives and determine to be ready for Him to return today – but it needs to go beyond that into the mundane things of everyday life. In Jesus' parable, it was when the wicked servant realised that his master *wasn't* returning today, that his conduct went down hill[2]. I once asked a group of Christians what they would do if they knew that Jesus was returning today and they gave me many different answers but none like the one Peter gives in his first letter: "The end of all things is near. *Therefore* be clear-minded and self-controlled so that you can pray"[3]. He then gives further practical advice which is well worth reading, but his first point is to have a clear head! Don't rely on an emotional response to a message about Jesus returning – but think it through. What changes will we make in our lives? How will we re-organise them so that prayer becomes more prominent?

The writer to the Hebrews encourages us to "run *with perseverance* the race marked out for us" (it's a marathon rather than a quick sprint) but he goes on to remind us that

---

[1] 2 Pet 3:11-14
[2] Matt 24:48-49
[3] 1 Pet 4:7

Jesus endured the cross "for the joy set before Him"[1]. He was looking to the future, which enabled Him to endure the present, and there is no better example than Jesus.

And finally...

In closing, here is a brief message for anyone reading this book who has never repented of their sin and put their faith in the Lord Jesus Christ.

When Paul was preaching in Athens he told the crowd "God... now commands all people everywhere to repent. For *He has set a day when He will judge the world* with justice by the Man He has appointed. He has given proof of this to all men by raising Him from the dead"[2].

Jesus is that Man who rose from the dead, and His day is approaching when He will return and judge the world. For those of us who know Him, that day is a wonderful and certain hope, but for others it will be a terrible experience. The book of Revelation speaks about "the wrath of the Lamb"[3] which seems incongruous since a lamb is the gentlest of animals. Jesus is called "the Lamb" because, like the lambs in the Old Testament, He was sacrificed for sin and, offering no resistance, He went to the Cross to pay the penalty due to us ... but the next time He comes will be very different and we will see the wrath of the Lamb as never before. Call out to Him today before it is too late.

---

[1] Heb 12:1-2
[2] Acts 17:30-31
[3] Rev 6:16

Lo! He comes with clouds descending,
Once for favoured sinners slain;
Thousand thousand saints attending,
Swell the triumph of His train:
Hallelujah! Hallelujah!
God appears on earth to reign.

Every eye shall now behold Him
Robed in dreadful majesty;
Those who set at naught and sold Him,
Pierced and nailed Him to the tree,
Deeply wailing, deeply wailing,
Shall the true Messiah see.

Now redemption, long expected,
See in solemn pomp appear;
All His saints, by man rejected,
Now shall meet Him in the air:
Hallelujah! Hallelujah!
See the day of God appear!

Those dear tokens of His passion
Still His dazzling body bears;
Cause of endless exultation
To His ransomed worshippers;
With what rapture, with what rapture
Gaze we on those glorious scars!

Yea, Amen! let all adore Thee,
High on Thine eternal throne;
Saviour, take the power and glory,
Claim the kingdom for Thine own;
O come quickly! O come quickly!
Everlasting God, come down![1]

---

[1] Charles Wesley (1758)

- Appendix A -

The pre-post debate

Apart from my deeply held conviction about the truth of "pre-millennialism" (the view I expounded in Chapter 4, that Jesus will reign on Earth for 1000 years after He returns), I have tried to avoid controversial issues in the main body of the book but that doesn't mean I don't consider them important, or that I don't have any views about these matters. These appendices are for those who want to know more – but please don't get so engrossed in them that you forget the main message of this book!

The great tribulation

Apart from the different views about the Millennium, the other main area of controversy concerns the period immediately *prior* to the Second Coming, known as the "tribulation" or "great tribulation". These terms are used in Scripture[1], plus there are many other passages that don't use these words but are commonly believed to refer to this period. The length of the tribulation is usually believed to be seven years (although some think it is only 3½ years) – but that's going beyond the scope of this appendix. The main point is that this period (or at least a part of it) will be so dreadful that, to quote Jesus, "if those days had not been cut short, no-one would survive"[2].

---

[1] Matt 24:21,29; Rev 7:14

[2] Matt 24:22

Will Christians go through it?

There is a widely held belief that Christians will not be on Earth during the tribulation but will be "snatched away" when Jesus returns unseen by the world, coming only as far as somewhere in the sky, where all the Christians on Earth will meet Him and accompany Him back to heaven. After the tribulation Jesus will return visibly – so it could be said there are three comings of Christ, but the middle one doesn't count because He won't actually reach the Earth (this is often called His "coming *for* the church").

The above belief is called "pre-tribulationism" (or "pre-trib" for short), i.e. Christians will be removed *before* the tribulation) whereas my view that Christians will remain on Earth and Jesus will not return at all until the end of this period, is called "post-trib". There is also "mid-trib" – the belief that Christians will be removed in the middle of the tribulation, or even in stages throughout the tribulation period!

Let me just clarify that this is independent of the millennial issue, so you could be post-trib and pre-millennial, pre-trib and amillennial (not believing in a literal Millennium at all), and so on – but this appendix is just about the pre- and post-trib debate. I won't pretend this is anything like a thorough examination of the topic – and I'm not aiming to prove my belief – but some may be interested to know how I arrived at it.

My experience

Before I started my 15-month period of Bible study when I was 17, I had heard Christians talk about Jesus returning to Earth – but with very little detail, and I am certain I had never heard any of the "pre" or "post" arguments. Being convinced I should read nothing except the Bible itself meant I was *unhindered by pre-conceived ideas* – and throughout my Christian life I've found that to be a wonderful position. Even when we are convinced about a particular doctrine, something may come along that shakes our belief and, whenever this has happened to me, I've found it really exciting to systematically work through the Scriptures and discover what they really say. We should, of course, always try to do that but, when we have pre-conceived ideas, it is amazing how easily we can skip over the passages that seem to contradict our beliefs and dwell on those that don't.

Another hindrance to unbiased study is using a Bible that has embedded notes – which is very different to reading separate books and commentaries. Although I didn't use the latter during those 15 months (and very rarely since), I have no objection to others doing so but would strongly warn against using Bibles with embedded articles and notes. The problem with these volumes is that as soon as you read a verse and before you've had the chance to even think about it, you look at the notes and say to yourself "so that's what it means"! Subsequently, you may not even remember what you read in the Scriptures themselves and what you read in the notes, let alone be open to other interpretations.

During my initial studies, I read nothing that made me think Christians would be removed from the Earth before the tribulation, and the thought never even entered my head. This certainly doesn't mean it can't be true because there have been numerous occasions on which I have re-read a familiar passage of Scripture and exclaimed "I've never seen that before" (perhaps you have had that experience)!

Although I don't assume I couldn't have missed something, I would, however, expect to be able to see it when someone else points it out – but this hasn't been the case with pre-trib teaching. The first time I came across this view was in a Christian magazine – and I was completely astonished because it rang no bells with anything I had read in Scripture. I wrote to the author asking how he had reached this conclusion (little knowing his view was very common) and he graciously replied – but his arguments appeared so flimsy that I assumed it was just a quirky idea held by him alone and I soon forgot about it!

In the ensuing years, however, I became increasingly aware that the pre-trib view was widely held and, following some discussions with friends, one of them suggested I should read a very detailed exposition of this view by a well-known scholar. I prayed about this and, feeling the purpose of not reading books about the Second Coming had been fulfilled, went ahead and read it. I could see where some of the ideas came from but, when I finished the book, was amazed that anyone could build an important doctrine from inferences as opposed to clear statements. Some exponents have even admitted that pre-trib teaching cannot be found plainly in Scripture but can be read between the lines! Personally, I am doubtful if anyone would find it if they hadn't already been taught it but, once an idea is fixed in our minds, we tend to interpret everything we read in that light. So, if it isn't explicitly stated in Scripture, where did this pre-trib teaching come from?

Popularity of pre-tribulationism

There is no record of any specific pre-trib teaching before the year 1830 when a lady called Margaret McDonald gave a prophecy stating that the Second Coming would be accomplished in two stages – but from there the teaching spread with amazing speed in the Western world. It was taken up by the influential English Bible teacher John Nelson Darby who took it to the USA and convinced Cyrus Scofield, compiler of the Scofield Bible. This Bible was one of the first to contain embedded explanatory notes and it became very popular – no longer did readers need to search the Scriptures for themselves to discover its teachings or look things up in separate commentaries – they could simply look at the notes on the same page and see what the passage meant. I've already expressed my view on such publications and can't help wondering if they violate the solemn warning in Revelation not to add anything to the prophecy of this book[1].

In modern times, the pre-trib view has been further popularised (or perhaps we should say "sensationalised") by many novels and films about unbelievers suddenly discovering their Christian friends and family have disappeared, often with disastrous results such as an aeroplane crashing because the pilot was a believer! It is a sad commentary on the church of today that some believers are more ready to accept what they see at a cinema than what it says in the Bible.

I realise this may sound harsh – and I do know there are many diligent and respected Bible scholars who hold this view, but I believe it needs to be challenged.

---

[1] Rev 22:18

Some passages to read

Many Christians think this topic is too complex for the "ordinary believer" to understand, so we have to rely on "experts". I don't for one moment question the fact that Christ has given teachers to the church[1] and that this is a vital ministry – however many years we have read the Bible, there will still be much we don't understand, and the insights of others are often very helpful – but, having said this, there is a huge amount that almost anyone can understand.

Let's take, for example, two substantial passages which speak of the rise of an evil and oppressive regime prior to the return of Christ – Daniel 7 in the Old Testament and Matthew 24 in the New. I urge you to read these for yourselves and see if you are left with the impression that Christians won't be on Earth when this happens.

In Daniel 7, the prophet saw this regime "waging war against the saints and defeating them" and a ruler emerging from it who "will speak against the Most High and oppress His saints... *the saints will be handed over to him*..."[2] – no suggestion of them being snatched away.

In Matthew 24, Jesus quotes Daniel, and speaks about a terrible time unequalled in history but, rather than saying the elect will be snatched away before all this, He says the days will be shortened for their sake[3]. Like Daniel, Jesus describes one dramatic and very public event: "as lightning that comes from the east is visible even in the west, so will be the coming of the Son of Man". There is no suggestion

---

1 Eph 4:11

2 Dan 7:19-25

3 Matt 24:15-23

here of any "secret event" or that this is part 2 of a two-stage coming – in fact He warns against those who point to a coming not seen by all... "if anyone tells you 'There he is, out in the desert,' do not go out; or, 'Here he is, in the inner rooms', do not believe it". Jesus continues "all the nations of the Earth will mourn. They will see the Son of Man coming on the clouds of the sky, with great power and glory. And He will send His angels with a loud trumpet call, and they will *gather His elect* from the four winds, from one end of the heavens to the other"[1]. On more than one occasion, young Christians who *had* heard pre-trib teaching read the above chapter and came to me saying "where does this view come from? Jesus seems to say the exact opposite!".

One book you will probably find harder to understand is Revelation ... but just try Chapter 14, where John describes "the beast" and a regime that sounds like the one we read about in Daniel and Matthew. John ends his description with the comment "this calls for patient endurance on the part of the saints who obey God's commandments and remain faithful to Jesus"[2] – so they don't seem to have been snatched away.

It is in Paul's letters to the Thessalonians that pre-trib exponents find verses to support their teaching, but I cannot see any that clearly state it. On the other hand, Paul begins his second letter by addressing those who were suffering and describes a time when God "will give relief to you who are troubled" ... *not* when the Christians are secretly snatched away, but "this will happen when the

---

[1] Matt 24:26-31
[2] Rev 14:9-12

Lord Jesus is revealed from heaven in blazing fire with His powerful angels"[1].

I realise, of course, that I could justly be accused of being selective and simplistic but it's not my aim to prove my case – I want you to read the Scriptures for yourself and see what impression you get and, if you want to take it further, there are plenty of books to read on both sides of the argument.

Before I end this chapter, however, I will comment on just one frequently quoted phrase.

A thief in the night

Pre-trib exponents often say that Jesus will come like "a thief in the night" (also the title of a popular film about the event[2]) – Jesus Himself used the analogy[3], as did Paul[4] and Peter[5]. This has led people to believe that just like a burglar breaks into a house in the middle of the night and steals all the valuables downstairs while the owners are sound asleep upstairs, so Jesus will snatch away His church from this world, and the unbelievers will suddenly realise we have all disappeared.

The problem is that burglary is a modern concept, virtually unknown to people in New Testament times. As in many poor countries today, only the very rich had separate living and sleeping accommodation – most homes were only one-storey high with a flat roof, and people went to sleep

---

[1] 2 Thes 1:5-7

[2] written by J.Grant, directed by D.W. Thompson (1973)

[3] Matt 24:43-44

[4] 1 Thes 5:2

[5] 2 Pet 3:10

around the fire in the room where they had earlier cooked and eaten their meals. The chances of someone slipping in and stealing something unnoticed by any member of the household or by their neighbours was fairly remote!

If we want to know how Jesus understood the term "thief", we should remember His words "the thief comes only to steal and kill and destroy"[1] – and in His parable of the good Samaritan, He describes how thieves stripped their victim of his clothes, beat him and went away, leaving him half dead[2]. We have come to equate "thief" with "burglar", but the Biblical thief is better understood as a bandit.

The point about these references is *not* therefore that Jesus will come to the world *unseen*, but that He will come *unexpectedly*. Jesus confirms this understanding when He says "If the owner of the house had known at what time of night the thief was coming, he would have kept watch and would not have let his house be broken into"[3]. Paul, having used the same analogy of the thief, clearly states to his Christian readers "*but you*, brothers, are not in darkness so that this day should surprise you like a thief"[4] – although he does then warn them to be alert.

Am I saying therefore, that Jesus won't return for at least seven (or 3½) years, i.e. after the tribulation? That will be the topic of the next appendix…

---

1 John 10:10

2 Luke 10:30

3 Matt 24:43

4 1 Thes 5:4

- Appendix B -

Could Jesus return today?

There is a popular view among Christians that Jesus could return any moment – maybe today.

For some this literally means *any* moment, i.e. it *could* be today, but it could equally well be in 10,000 years' time – we simply don't know. Others, however, think there is a *very real possibility* He could return today because they believe the *signs* given in Scripture indicate the event is very near – and it is this second idea I am considering in this appendix.

Can we know the answer?

As soon as we start talking about predicting dates, some will quote Jesus' words "But about that day or hour *no one knows*, not even the angels in heaven, nor the Son, but only the Father", or "... you do not know on what day your Lord will come" or "the Son of Man will come at an hour when you do not expect Him"[1]. This last statement even suggests that whenever we think He is coming, we will be wrong! But is that the whole story?

First, we need to realise that, in the very same discourse where Jesus says all the above, He gives many signs for us to look out for and then says "when you see all these things, you know that it is near, *right at the door*"[2] (some

---

[1] Matt 24:36-44
[2] Matt 24:33

translations read "He is near"). One possibility here is that, although we cannot know the day and the hour, maybe we can know the year, or even the month or the week. If this is the case, however, Jesus' words suggest we can only be so certain when we are right on the verge of His return – but that is exactly what some people are claiming is the case.

Second, Jesus' statement about His return at an unexpected time is followed by a parable about faithful and wicked servants, and Jesus says of the latter "the master of *that* servant will come on a day when he does not expect him", whereas the faithful servant was ready at all times[1]. This is confirmed in Paul's first letter to the Thessalonians when he first says "you know very well that the day of the Lord will come like a thief in the night. While people are saying 'Peace and safety', destruction will come on them suddenly, as labour pains on a pregnant woman, and they will not escape" – which seems to back up the idea that Jesus will come unexpectedly – but Paul then says "But *you* are not in darkness so that this day should surprise you like a thief"[2]. Again, in his second letter to the same church, he gives specific signs to watch out for, and even says at one point "that day will *not come until...*"[3] so, for those Christians it certainly wasn't the case that He could return at any moment. Neither Paul nor Peter expected this – Paul wrote to Timothy about things that would happen in the future[4], and both men wrote that the time of their death was approaching[5].

---

[1] Matt 24:45-51

[2] 1 Thes 5:1-4

[3] 2 Thes 2:3

[4] 1 Tim 4:1; 2 Tim 3:1-9

[5] 2 Tim 4:6; 2 Pet 1:14

So, all this convinces me that the return of Jesus is dependent on the fulfilment of signs which we *can* and *should* study – but do they indicate that He could return this year, for example?

General and specific signs

Some of the signs, such as earthquakes, wars, increase of lawlessness, and many others, are *general*. Sceptics will be quick to say that in every generation people have observed such things and thought the end was near – and to some extent I agree – but I am struck by Jesus' words "You *will hear* of wars and rumours of wars... there will be famines and earthquakes *in various places*"[1]. In the past, a disaster occurred somewhere, and the local believers thought "that's it! Jesus is about to return" (just as all of us are prone to be influenced by our own narrow experience) but, unlike those previous generations, we can now see what is happening *worldwide* – and I believe this overview shows these general predictions being fulfilled on an increasing scale.

There are also some very specific signs. For example, from my understanding of Scripture, Jesus couldn't have returned before the Jews were back in their own land, ready to gaze on the One they pierced[2] – something which started to be fulfilled in 1948. Another specific sign to which we have already alluded is found in Paul's reference to the day of Jesus' return not coming *until the man of sin is revealed*[3] (the "man of sin" is usually considered to be

---

[1] Matt 24:6-7
[2] Zech 12:10
[3] 2 Thes 2:3

the same as “the beast”[1] or “the antichrist”[2]). Whether we think Jesus could return very soon therefore depends on how we view this and other related prophecies, especially those in the book of Revelation…

The man of sin

Among those who hold a specific view on how to interpret Revelation, there are three main schools of thought. What follows are very simplistic definitions because there are variations in all the views – but I believe this gives the general idea …

- *Preterist*. Most of Revelation was fulfilled in the first century AD. The man of sin was Nero, or some other Roman emperor and the “end of the age” was the destruction of Jerusalem.

- *Historicist*. Revelation covers the whole of history from Jesus’ first coming to His return, and the man of sin is the papacy, especially in the period that popes held civil power.

- *Futurist*. Most of Revelation is still to happen. The man of sin is an individual who will rule the whole world during the Tribulation. This view is *by far* the majority one, and it is very rare to encounter preterist or historicist teaching.

From this, we can see that the man of sin prophecy is no barrier to preterists and historicists believing Jesus could

---

[1] Rev 13:1-8
[2] 1 John 2:18

return very soon, since they believe it has already been fulfilled... but how can a futurist say this when they are expecting an individual to rule the whole world first? And, given that this is the majority view, why do so many Christians say the return of Christ could happen at any moment? The answer of course, as we explained in Appendix A, is that most futurists believe in a pre-tribulation rapture so, like the preterist and the historicist, they *can* say they believe Jesus could return today (by which they mean His return for the church, *not* the event visible to all). I question, however, whether this is true, even from a pre-tribulation perspective...

In order to believe that Jesus will return for His church today, a pre-tribulation adherent would need to believe that a world dictator will be in place tomorrow to mark the start of the tribulation – but is that realistic? I certainly know world events can change very fast which is why, even from my post-tribulation perspective, I believe Jesus might return in my lifetime – but could a world dictator seize power overnight? Some believers (in both the pre- and post-tribulation camps) believe the references to the man of sin ruling over the whole world refer only to the "Roman world", i.e. Europe, but even if we accept this view, could that happen tomorrow? I leave my pre-tribulation friends to ponder that question.

The fact that my theology is incompatible with believing that Jesus could return today has never troubled me much because, as stated earlier, neither Peter nor Paul believed Jesus would return before they died – but that doesn't mean they weren't ready. There is, however, one last twist to this story...

Multiple fulfilments of prophecy

I have already explained how I reached my post-tribulation beliefs through months of Bible study. Something else I concluded in those days was that Biblical prophecies are often fulfilled multiple times, with each fulfilment getting bigger – and many Old Testament events pre-shadow greater fulfilments.

A striking example of this is found in prophecies regarding Solomon, already mentioned in Chapter 4. Old Testament statements such as "I will be his Father and he will be My son"[1], and much of Psalm 72, originally related to Solomon – but he is a "type" or "pre-shadowing" of Jesus.

Another example of multiple fulfilment is found in the final verse of Malachi, which says that God will send Elijah before the great and terrible day of the Lord[2]. Most people assume this was completely fulfilled by John the Baptist before the First Coming of Jesus, but Malachi's phraseology sounds more like the Second Coming. Jesus Himself, however, seems to indicate that both are correct – He first says "Elijah comes and *will restore* all things" but then says "Elijah *already came*"[3].

A few years after my studies, I first learned about the historicist view from my friend Alan, who had studied it for many years. Unlike my reaction to the pre-tribulation view, I *did* think it could be found in Scripture but saw it as an example of multi-fulfilment prophecies described above. I also see the preterist view in the same light, as it certainly does appear that many events leading up to the destruction

---

[1] 2 Sam 7:14

[2] Mal 4:5-6

[3] Matt 17:11-12

of Jerusalem foreshadow events at the end of the age. As well as examples already given, I believe this idea is borne out by John when he writes that "the antichrist *is coming*" but then says "even now many antichrists *have come*"[1].

If it wasn't the case that much of Revelation has been partially fulfilled in multiple ways throughout history, we would have to believe that God has given us very little information about the last 2000 years but extensive details about the final few before Jesus returns. This is possible, but seems somewhat unlikely and, if we hold the pre-tribulation view that we won't even be on Earth for those final years, it becomes less likely still.

My reserve belief

Having said all this, since hearing about the historicist view, I have kept it as a "reserve belief" when considering the main topic of this appendix. I want to leave room for being wrong and have sometimes appealed to this teaching (rather than pre-tribulation futurism) as a viable alternative – and I think this has stopped me becoming complacent in believing it will be quite a few years before Jesus returns.

In recent years, I have looked at historicism more closely, reading various books and articles on the subject – and must admit that, for a while, I began to wonder if my futurist view was wrong. Here are the main issues that caused me to waver:

a) The futurist view as taught today originates from a Jesuit theologian called Francisco Ribera (1537–1591),

---

[1] 1 John 2:18

who was seeking to divert attention from the historicist view that put the Roman Catholic church in such an unfavourable light. Although I don't rule out the possibility of there being some true believers inside the Roman Catholic church, I do view it as apostate, so this origin of futurist teaching troubled me.

b) Although I know the book of Revelation is highly symbolic, I previously considered some of the symbolism too dramatic to believe that the historicist interpretation could be its final fulfilment. For example, the *worldwide* power and total domination of the man of sin (or "the beast") is repeatedly stressed[1] but the historicist says this just refers to Papal power in the Roman empire. I have come to realise, however, that some Old Testament prophecies accepted as completely fulfilled also use very dramatic language – and even Luke speaks about *all the inhabited world* being taxed at the time of Jesus' birth[2] when he actually means the entire *Roman* world (as many modern translations state).

c) The historicist view has been popular for much of church history – held by many respected Christians – whereas futurism only became popular in the last couple of centuries. John Wycliffe, Martin Luther, John Calvin, Thomas Cranmer, John Knox, Jonathan Edwards, John Wesley and many others, all held the historicist view that the man of sin had already come in the form of the papal system. You can even find a reference to this view on the dedication page of the Authorised Version of the Bible (published in 1611)

---

[1] Rev 13:3, 7, 8, 16, 17

[2] Luke 2:1

where the translators refer to King James' defence of the Truth being "a blow unto that man of sin as will not be healed".

As I said in Appendix A, it can be a good thing when our firmly held beliefs are challenged and we re-examine them with an open mind – so this is what I did, and I will now explain my current thinking on the above.

Regarding the origins of futurist teaching: first, I didn't get my futurist view from Ribera or any other teacher but formed it from my own reading of the Scriptures. I don't think I would ever have reached the historicist view by that method – not because it can't be seen in Scripture, but because I don't have a very good knowledge of history. Whilst fully accepting that Bible study can be enhanced by great learning and scholarship, I have always taken the view that the most obvious interpretation is usually the correct one, and that much of our "digging deeper" is because we don't like what the Scriptures say at face value! There are exceptions of course, but I question whether something as important as the return of Christ, and the signs we are repeatedly told to watch for, would be so obscure to the "common man" as they are in the historicist interpretation. Coupled with the fact that we have cyclical historicists (believing that Revelation covers the same events several times over) and linear historicists (believing the book describes events just once, reading from start to finish) makes me wonder how many people could grasp this interpretation. I think I have more than average Bible knowledge but find it difficult to follow.

Second, although Ribera is regarded as the originator of futurism as taught today, some key features of it are found in the teachings of the church fathers. For example, Irenaeus (c.120-200 AD, taught by Polycarp who in turn was discipled by the Apostle John) believed that the man of sin would reign for a literal 3½ years in a literal temple in Jerusalem. Hippolytus (170-236 AD) also believed this and linked Daniel's "70th week"[1] to this period.

Regarding the very dramatic language sometimes used in Scripture for events already fulfilled, I have already said that many historicist interpretations may be valid, but that doesn't mean there cannot be a further fulfilment. Also relevant to this is whether we are right to have completely abandoned the historicist teachings of many respected Christians in past generations. I will readily acknowledge that in recent times there has been a huge departure from Biblical truth amongst Christians – and one of these has been a widespread acceptance of the Roman Catholic church as just another Christian denomination. In this regard, I believe the historicists were *right* and that Ribera's version of futurism (in which the apostasy of the Roman Catholic church plays no part) was *wrong*. In line with my belief that prophetic scriptures can be fulfilled multiple times, I think historicists of past centuries were right in much of what they saw, it was relevant to them, and *some of it is still relevant to us* ... but, as we get nearer the end of the age, the futurist interpretation becomes more relevant.

So – could Jesus return today? According to my post-tribulation futurist theology – no... but I can't be 100% certain, so I have to say "Maybe He could"!

---

[1] Dan 9:27

All of this makes me even more sure of the most important truth – that we must always hold the hope of Jesus returning before us, and remain faithful until the end.

Printed in Great Britain
by Amazon

59440059R00059